To Connor, Sydney, Harper, Isaac, Claire & Abigail. My constant reminders that this world contains true joy and wonder.

"Wow! One always expects fantastic insights from Shaun Belding, but this book brings the concepts of customer experience and customer loyalty to an entirely new level.

Member experience is the lifeblood of success in our business, and making sure we are on top of our game is what continues to allow us to grow our amazing brand. *The Journey to WOW* is going to be a critical part of our strategy as we continue to make a positive and healthy impact on our members lives."

—LESLIE W. DALEY, Chief Learning & People Resource Officer, Orangetheory Fitness

"Shaun Belding's *The Journey to WOW* was a treat to read. The topic of customer experience can sometimes by dry and formulaic, but Shaun understands that we are all storytellers and so the most effective way to convey important insights is through a well-written story. The difference between perfection and excellence; the importance of delivering consistently high service; being congruent in your brand and understanding that an outstanding customer journey is a never-ending process for the provider; all of those insights are woven tightly inside an engaging character-driven narrative.

This book should be required reading for everyone in the customer experience space, except homework has never been so enjoyable."

—DAVE CARROLL, Singer-Songwriter and creator of United Breaks Guitars

"An insightful read—Belding's method of delivering an excellent customer experience highlights the opportunity all organizations have to win with customer loyalty."

—ROSS GARRETSON, Vice President, Customer Experience Hunter Douglas North America

"Each year I read thousands of perspectives on customer experience, customer service, and how to delight customers. *The Journey to WOW* ties these concepts together and delivers a 'wow' of its own—an entertaining story! Read it and put the insights to work to improve your customer relationships."

—**BOB THOMPSON**, Founder/CEO of CustomerThink, Author of *Hooked On Customers: The Five Habits of Legendary Customer-Centric Companies*

"Customers do not rave about a company that merely meets their expectations. And while they may be satisfied, that does not mean they are loyal. Moreover, dissatisfied customers, equipped with the megaphone of social media, can rant to the world how bad you are to do business with. So how do you create an outstanding customer experience that drives real customer loyalty?

One of my favorite quotes is from Samuel Johnson, 'People need to be reminded more than they need to be instructed.' In a very entertaining storytelling format, *The Journey to WOW* offers a Don't and Do guide for customer journey mapping, and serves as a valuable reminder to managers—and especially C-suite executives—not to lose sight that it is always about the customer's experience, not theirs."

—**BILL QUISENG**, Customer Service Expert/Speaker/Blogger

"If you are looking to go from now to WOW, check out Shaun Belding's book, *The Journey to WOW*. Shaun creatively shares a story, lessons learned and creates a relatable environment for you to grow your business. His dedication to WOW'ing his readers is evidenced by his ability to translate the sometimes complex process of improving the customer experience. If you want to increase your customer loyalty and better your customer experience, go no further than this book of WOW. Well done Shaun!"

—**DOUG SANDLER**, Co-host of The Nice Guys on Business Podcast, Author of *Nice Guys Finish First*

The Journey to WOW:
A Roadmap to Outstanding
Customer Experience
and Loyalty

by Shaun Belding

ISBN 978-1-63393-693-5

Published by

 köehlerbooks™

210 60th Street
Virginia Beach, VA 23451
800-435-4811
www.koehlerbooks.com

THE JOURNEY TO
WOW

A ROADMAP TO OUTSTANDING
CUSTOMER EXPERIENCE
AND LOYALTY

SHAUN BELDING

VIRGINIA BEACH
CAPE CHARLES

FOREWORD

IT'S NO SECRET that the customer experience has become a focus for the executives and owners who lead companies. It's the dominant driver of organization success. It is what differentiates one company from its competition. It is what gets a customer to want to come back. It is what makes a customer want to tell their friends and colleagues. It is the essence of what creates customer loyalty and makes a company memorable. So, if everyone knows it, then why is it that so many organizations seem to struggle in their efforts to create consistently amazing customer experiences? Why isn't everyone amazing?

Because creating a customer-centric culture isn't easy. There are a lot of moving parts. It requires skilled people and strong, focused and empowered leadership. It takes persistence and, most importantly, it takes a very good plan.

The Journey to WOW nails it.

Shaun Belding tells a delightful story that points out the many opportunities to deliver that WOW to a customer. Along the way you'll learn, through many examples, how WOW builds relationships. In some cases, WOW may mean an "over-the-top" experience, while other times it's just something small—something that stands out because an employee was thoughtful. Yet, in the end, it is a focus on the customer, not by one employee, but by an entire company of employees who understand how they can impact the customer's experience.

My personal definition of WOW—or amazing customer service, as I like to call it—resonates with this message. It isn't about being over the top all of the time. Typically, amazing service comes when you're above average—even just a little above average. But it must be consistent. The customer must know this is the experience they will always receive. And when they can say that, you will have achieved customer amazement —or WOW, as Shaun likes to say.

The Journey to WOW is a journey that everyone in every organization should go on. There is a lot of sound advice in this book, and more than a few "aha" moments. As a bonus, it's also a lot of fun to read.

Enjoy, and best of luck in your journey to WOW!

—SHEP HYKEN
Customer service expert and New York Times bestselling author of *The Amazement Revolution*

CHAPTER ONE

CAMERON WHITEHALL HAD A morning routine. Alarm at 6:00. Feet on the floor by 6:05. Showered by 6:20. Fed by 6:40. Out of the door by 7:00. Stuck in traffic by 7:03.

Cameron liked routine. It gave him a sense of comfort and control, along with a little bit of superstitious satisfaction that the day ahead was going to be manageable. Routine gave him something to grasp when things went sideways, a security blanket with which to greet the day. The only time, in fact, that routine didn't work for him was when the routine itself went sideways.

Which was, at the moment, exactly what was happening.

It was 4:00 am on March 27, and Cameron had already been awake for an hour. It wasn't helping that a seventy-six pound, three-year-old golden lab named Chewbacca had been staring at him from five inches away for the last ten minutes. Cameron turned his head and looked into the big, soft brown eyes. "Just because I'm awake early doesn't mean you get an early breakfast you know," he grumbled.

Hearing the word *breakfast*, Chewbacca barked, ran in a circle, then scampered out of the room and down the stairs.

Breakfast was not something to be missed. Cameron rolled over and stared at the ceiling. After a few minutes, he groaned and willed himself to stand, shuffled into the shower, and let the warm water wash away any remaining pretense of sleepiness.

Twenty minutes later, as Cameron was getting dressed, Chewbacca bounded back up the stairs and skidded to a stop at the bedroom doorway. He tilted his head and looked at Cameron. Perhaps Cameron had forgotten he'd mentioned breakfast? Cameron smiled as he pulled on his belt, inspecting himself in the full-length mirror to ensure everything was in order. "Maybe *you* can tell me why I haven't been able to sleep for the past two nights," he said to the dog. Sleep wasn't something he ever struggled with.

"It's just our normal Monday morning meeting." Cameron said to his reflection. "Why is *this* one bothering me?" And yet here he was, getting dressed at 4:30 in the morning. He couldn't shake the feeling of impending . . . something. Not doom. Nothing so dramatic. But something. He shook his head to clear his thoughts.

Chewbacca saw the headshake and interpreted this as *I'll be right down*, ran in another circle, and raced happily away back downstairs. Cameron watched him and smiled. Chewy never lost sleep. He was always happy, and never asked for much more than a little attention.

If only people were that simple, he thought.

Cameron made his way downstairs to find the lab anxiously waiting beside his bowl. He filled the dish and the dog's head dove in. "Now don't be expecting this every morning," he said. "And don't be expecting a second breakfast in another hour."

Chewy lifted his head briefly to look at Cameron.

Wow, two breakfasts.

CHAPTER TWO

THE DRIVE ALONG THE Long Beach Freeway to Vernon was pretty civilized at five o'clock in the morning. Twenty-five minutes instead of fifty-five minutes. *Might be worth considering a change in routine*, Cameron thought. *Who needs sleep anyway?*

Truth be told, it could be worse. Household Solutions Inc. could have put their head office right in downtown Los Angeles. Even though the difference in distance was a scant five miles, it could add an hour to the commute on a bad day.

As he drove, he thought about the upcoming meeting feeding his insomnia. There was really no reason to believe that it was going to be any different than other weekly executive team meetings. Same time, same people; and while the issues changed from week to week, the general topic was always the same—growing and building the business.

There was very little controversy, and few issues that were truly burning at Household Solutions. In fact, for a company its size, things were going remarkably well. But there was something about the email that landed in his inbox on Friday that had set off a tiny warning bell in Cameron's engineer brain. On the surface it seemed innocent enough. Just one sentence:

Hi:

Please set aside an additional 30 minutes for this Monday's meeting.

Thanks,
Gerard

Maybe it was the brevity. The CEO, Gerard Ogilvy, was known for his long and detailed missives. Maybe it was the extra half-hour, but their meetings often went well past their scheduled time. Cameron couldn't see how it could be bad news. The company's sales had been increasing at a steady pace of three to five percent every year. And, as Senior Vice President of Operations, responsible for manufacturing and new product development, he was pretty sure things on his end were moving quite smoothly.

In fact, as a direct result of initiatives he had spearheaded, costs were down, productivity was up, and they had successfully launched a record number of new products internationally. Cameron gave himself a mental slap. *Things are good. Why are you assuming the worst?*

The elevator doors opened to the fifth floor at 5:30, and it occurred to him that he was likely the first one in the office. He was going to have to figure out how to work that giant commercial coffee maker in the lunch room.

The lights in the hallway brightened in sequence as he walked past reception toward his office. Cameron loved that. The power saving, motion-activated device, which had been his idea, remained dim unless something was moving. But Cameron's favorite part was how the lights brightened progressively in front of you as you walked down the dim hallway, as if you were an office deity bringing enlightenment wherever you went. He smiled and began pointing at the lights as he walked, as though they brightened at his command.

The lunch room was on the way to his office, so he turned in to get the coffee started. The cleaners had been—everything was neat and in its place. But there was already one half-full pot on the burner. *Don't tell me they left this on all weekend,* Cameron thought. *Ew.*

He picked up the pot and walked to the sink to dump it. He stuck his nose in it just to be sure. It smelled quite fresh. He inhaled once more. It actually smelled remarkably good. Better than usual. He poured a little in a cup and sipped it. *Huh.* This was not the usual lunch-room coffee. Someone had obviously beaten him in this morning, and whoever it was got extra points for their coffee-making skills. He filled his cup and headed toward his office.

He saw the light glowing in Gerard Ogilvy's office just before he got to his own. *Aha!* Cameron thought. *Even the boss couldn't sleep. Well, no time like the present to remind him of how dedicated an employee you are.* He poked his head into the large, ornate oak-trimmed office. "Morning boss," he said cheerfully.

Gerard Ogilvy was founder and CEO of Household Solutions Inc. He was in his early sixties but looked closer to mid-forties. Tall, lanky, with thinning blond hair, Gerard looked more like a tenured university professor than a no-nonsense CEO. His undeniable charisma was marked with an easy-going grace and charm that inspired fierce loyalty among his employees— Cameron included.

At the sound of Cameron's voice, Gerard looked up with an expression of mild surprise. "Hey Cameron," he said with a smile, "what brings you in so early?"

"I heard there was good coffee on," Cameron replied, holding his mug up. "How about you? Can't sleep?"

"Slept like a baby," Gerard laughed. "But I'm always in around five. I find I can get a lot done in the extra few hours before the action begins around here. And I treat myself with a pot of fresh-ground Jamaican Blue Mountain Coffee."

"Which," he nodded toward Cameron's mug, "you seem to have discovered."

"Sorry," Cameron said, reddening a little. "I didn't realize this was your private stash."

Gerard waved his hand and laughed. "Don't worry. It's the least I can do for someone dedicated enough to show up for work this early in the morning." He punched a few keys on his keyboard and squinted at the screen. "So I'll see you at ten?" he asked, glancing up.

Cameron recognized his cue to leave, so he nodded and made his exit. Everything seemed fine, and if Gerard had some surprise for the upcoming meeting, it wasn't evident. He had spied a freshly bound document sitting on Gerard's large antique desk with a loose piece of paper partially covering it. He caught some of the title: "Household Solutions—*something*—Recommendation." Cameron didn't think much of it. Gerard always had a lot of things on the go. Besides, he hadn't seen anything about a recommendation on the meeting agenda.

And that's when it hit him. *Agenda.*

There had been no agenda attached to the email. That's what was so odd about it. There were always agendas for their meetings, even though they didn't change much. Why not this one? Gerard was a bear for detail, and that's the sort of detail he wouldn't likely miss. Cameron stopped and considered for a moment. Was it just a simple omission? Cameron looked at his watch. Five fifty-five. *Well, we'll find out in four hours, won't we?*

CHAPTER THREE

THE TIME BEGRUDGINGLY TICKED to ten o'clock. Cameron collected his notepad and papers that seemed relevant and refilled his coffee. A quick sniff confirmed they were back to the regular brand. One minute later, he took his usual seat in the boardroom.

The main boardroom of Household Solutions Inc. was impressive in both size and design. It could be divided into three separate meeting rooms, or combined into a single room capable of seating almost three hundred people. The dozen sixty-inch LED monitors somehow didn't appear out of place in the elegant cherry and tiger wood décor.

The electronics in the room were state-of-the-art, much of it designed by Household Solutions engineers. A hotline connected to key people in each of the primary business units. If a question came up in a meeting, no one had to wait. They could go straight to the source. Twenty people around the world carried dedicated cell phones, prepared for those very calls.

There was video conferencing, of course. But even that had a twist. Embedded in the boardroom table, in front of each seat, were small printers/scanners. When someone in an office in Atlanta, for example, wanted to distribute a document during a meeting, they simply fed it into their scanner. The report would appear in front of meeting participants in other cities.

Every meeting was video-recorded and stored. When someone wanted to refer back to something, they could. Important decisions and action items were tagged and indexed to find quickly. Tone and nuances weren't lost this way.

The best part—at least according to Cameron—was that each room was equipped with electronic signal blocking to prevent the use and abuse of wireless devices. The whole environment was designed to enhance communication while minimizing distractions.

They used only one of the three rooms for today's meeting, although it was still a large space for the seven people who would sit at just one end of the table. Cameron looked around. Gerard's seat was still empty.

Gerard always sat at the head of the table. The rest of the seating order fell in line with the pecking order. Chief Financial Officer Gayle Humphries and Chief Operating Officer Syd Rosen sat immediately to Gerard's left and right. Then came the senior vice presidents. Next to Gayle was Finance SVP Will Abbot and Human Resources SVP Susan Tremmel. Next to Syd sat Marketing SVP Stan Tetu and Cameron.

Cameron thought of the seating order as an interesting social phenomenon. It's not like it was pre-assigned. No one had ever insisted on a certain placement. It just sort of happened that way. He often wondered how the others would react if he sat in a different place, just for fun.

For the most part, everyone around the table got along well, and Cameron liked all of them. This wasn't surprising. They had each been hand-selected by Gerard, and all shared at least some of Gerard's qualities—a good sense of humor, a strong work ethic, and tremendous competence. It was, in fact, the strongest leadership team Cameron had ever worked with.

The only personality clash he had, if you could even call it that, was with Stan Tetu. He liked Stan. He was bright, gregarious, and knew his stuff. But Cameron always felt that Stan was, in some way, competing with him. It wasn't overt. Just a whole bunch of little things that kept coming up. It didn't really make a lot of sense to Cameron. He and Stan couldn't be further apart when it came to disciplines. There just wasn't anything to compete *for*.

As Cameron finished up the last gulp of coffee, Gerard entered the room with an attractive, blonde, thirtyish woman following close behind. Her pressed gray and white ensemble and the Gucci portfolio screamed lawyer or consultant. It was a contrast to Gerard's unique look, which everyone referred to as professional disheveled. The woman wasn't familiar to Cameron. Judging by curious looks, they didn't recognize her, either.

Gerard spoke a few quiet words to her, then turned to the group. "My apologies for the delay, folks," he began. "I would like to introduce Emily Seaborne, a senior consultant for the JMB Group. She has some information to share with us." Heads turned and looked at each other. This was coming as a surprise to everyone. Cameron wasn't sure what to think. On the one hand, he was happy to see that his spidey sense still worked. On the other hand, this unexpected stranger was a little disconcerting.

"A while back, I asked JMB to take a critical look at our company," Gerard continued, deliberately making eye contact with each of the leadership team. "Although everything seems to be going quite well, I had a nagging feeling we were missing something. We're a pretty positive team here, which is a good thing. But there is always the risk of becoming a little too close to see objectively. I was concerned that we might be guilty of, shall we say, blowing some sunshine up our collective shorts."

Emily Seaborne remained expressionless, but her eyes shifted from Gerard to the group and back again. *Gauging our response to potential criticism,* Cameron thought.

"So this is where Ms. Seaborne comes in." Gerard reached over and switched on the controller for the multimedia center. "For the last three months her team has been looking at our company from a number of different angles, and I think you will be as interested as I in her rather inescapable conclusions. I have asked her to be blunt and straightforward and try to avoid that sugar-coating thing that consultants like to do." He glanced at Seaborne, whose lips pursed into the hint of a grin. "Quite frankly, she's pretty good at being blunt and straightforward, so if she happens to offend any of you, well . . ." he paused and grinned at the group. "Tough." The laughter around the room had a nervous edge.

Cameron sat back in his chair and crossed his arms. *Bring it on,* he thought. *Whatever she's got, I can handle.*

Without any further introduction, Gerard came around the table beside Susan Tremmel, across from Cameron. He flashed Cameron a grin and a wink as he sat. *What the heck was that all about?* Cameron thought. Suddenly, he was nervous, too.

"Thank you, Mr. Ogilvy," Seaborne began, then turned to the group. "I will be direct, I promise. And I apologize in advance if I tread on anyone's toes." She paused for a moment to put up a title slide on the center screen.

Household Solutions Inc. Recovery Recommendation.

Eyebrows rose in unison around the room. *Recovery? What do we need recovering from?*

Seaborne squared herself to the group and leaned forward so that her fingertips were touching the table in front of her. "I've got good news and bad news," she said deliberately.

Cameron's insides fluttered. *This is it,* he thought.

"The bad news is that Household Solutions Inc. is in a lot of trouble."

CHAPTER FOUR

THE ROOM WENT ABSOLUTELY silent, and the temperature dropped to sub-zero. Cameron felt as though he could actually hear the thoughts of those around him. Skepticism, mistrust, irritation. *The woman picked the wrong group to play this game with,* he thought. He had seen this consultant tactic before—drop a bombshell to get people's attention, and then show them the way to salvation. He could see how the approach might work with a group of closed-minded executives who were only focused on their own job security, but this team was different. There was a lot of pride in this room. This had better be good.

A quick glance at Gerard, however, told Cameron it would be. The CEO sat back in his chair, one leg crossed, hands loosely in his lap. He looked relaxed, but his eyes, directed exclusively at Seaborne, burned with fierce intensity. He had already heard this, Cameron realized, and believed it. Cameron's respect for the gregarious and charismatic CEO was unqualified. He had an uncanny sense for people, and his batting average was irrefutable. If Gerard thought what Seaborne had to say was important, it probably was.

"I know that sounds very dramatic," Seaborne continued, not wavering from the cynical eyes focused on her. "And I can assure you that I'm not playing the consultant game of 'drop a bombshell to get people's attention, and then show them the way to salvation.'" Cameron blinked. "Yet the truth is, the path Household Solutions is on is a scary one. Hopefully I can demonstrate this. More importantly, I hope I can demonstrate the good news—that you still have a lot of options in front of you. One of which, I believe, has a tremendous upside for the company."

No change in the temperature. *Enough of the preamble,* came the silent thoughts in unison. *You've got our attention. We're listening. Show us what you've got.* Seaborne picked up the remote and brought up a slide showing a five-year snapshot of the company.

"As you know, annual sales increases for the company have been consistently between three percent and five percent per year. Profits and EBITDA have mirrored this. On the surface, things look solid, but the numbers are deceptive." The next slide showed an exploding pie chart. "Even when you look at the business by product category, it would seem that each category is growing and profitable." Nods around the table. They had all seen these numbers before.

The next slide showed two exploding pie charts side-by-side. "The story changes, however," Seaborne continued, "when you look at overall sales and profitability by *product*." Cameron leaned forward and listened intently. She was in his territory now. Seaborne proceeded to lead them through a series of charts. As she did, the mood in the room progressed from skepticism, to consideration, to interest, to concern. By the time she was summarizing, no one doubted the validity of her conclusions.

"As you've seen," Seaborne concluded, "in every category, all of the real growth has come exclusively from the introduction of new product innovations. Sales of existing products are flat at best. The real story, though, comes when you compare the performance of existing products with the overall performance of their categories in the marketplace. Each of the categories are currently growing at a fairly rapid pace—between five percent and fifteen percent per year. Comparatively speaking, therefore, with our sales remaining flat while the market segments are growing, Household Solutions products are, for all intents and purposes, in *decline*."

"What is happening is simple. You are launching new products and gaining the initial hit in sales and margin. As your competitors begin to introduce comparable products with lower prices, stronger marketing, and greater distribution, they are quickly taking away your market share."

"The reality is that a couple of failed new-product launches in a row is all it will take for the company to be in serious trouble. You've been fortunate so far in that regard, but the odds are against your success rate staying as high as it is." She turned her head to acknowledge Cameron. "No offense intended," she said. Cameron nodded. She was right, and everyone knew it.

"It seems to me," Stan Tetu jumped in, "that this is simply a matter of controlling our production costs better." Cameron held back a scowl as he turned to the marketing vice president seated beside him. "If we used more offshore production—something I've been advocating for years, by the way—we would be able to compete better in the marketplace," Tetu continued. "My sales teams are up against lower-priced competitors every day and getting their butts kicked. Yes, our quality is better and we've tried to position ourselves that way, but both company buyers and the consumers out there are price-driven. Lower the production cost, then lower our prices. Then we can get some of this ground back."

Seaborne nodded to Tetu and looked around the room. Cameron flushed. He could throttle Tetu, although right now it was hard to argue with him. Household Solutions' products were priced at a premium—an inevitability of their higher quality. Cameron's team had investigated more offshore production options but had yet to find a way to ensure the quality they required.

Seaborne nodded and spoke haltingly, choosing her words with care. "Initially, that's what we thought, too," she said, "but that approach would really only postpone the inevitable." She paused, as if searching for words.

"You see," she continued, "what I have described so far are just symptoms. And the solution you suggest would certainly alleviate the symptoms . . . for a little while. But because there is a deeper, more systemic, underlying issue, it wouldn't work for long."

She cleared her throat gently and took a sip of water. "I promised I'd be direct, so here it is in plain English," she said, quietly surveying the room.

"It's not that you're too expensive," Seaborne said finally. "That's not why people stop buying from you. People stop buying from you because . . . well . . . because they don't like you."

The room erupted. Seaborne stood quietly as incredulity and anger filled the room. Gerard held out a hand, and everyone fell silent. "Folks," he said, "you've listened this far. You might as well hear her out to the end."

Cameron interjected. "But Gerard," he said, "it's ridiculous." He turned to still-silent Seaborne. "No offense intended." She nodded.

"We have an ongoing Voice-of-the-Customer survey to measure satisfaction levels," Cameron said defiantly. "The responses are generally outstanding. We're not perfect, but there certainly isn't any indication that our customers 'don't like us!'" Nods of agreement around the table.

Gerard contemplated Cameron for a moment, then turned to Seaborne. "Continue," he said quietly.

"It is true what you say about your Voice-of-the-Customer survey," Seaborne acknowledged to Cameron. Then reaching for the remote again she said to the group: "Unfortunately, it's not asking the right questions." She pushed a button, and the results from an entirely different survey filled all twelve screens.

"Your survey asked customers how satisfied they were with your *products*, to which the response was extremely positive. There is no question that consumers believe you have the best range of products on the market. We conducted a survey of our own, however, to find out how well customers like your *company*. The results of this research, as you can see, tell quite a different story."

Seaborne had everyone's attention again. "We surveyed two primary customer groupings. The first was the end consumer. The second was your distribution channels—retailers, wholesalers, etc. Here are the findings." She walked to the screen on the far right. "On a scale of one to ten, with ten being high, your distribution channels rate Household Solutions Inc. an average of 3.7 as a company they like doing business with. Consumers give you a 4.3."

She walked to the next screen. "Here are some of the descriptive words the distribution channel used to describe Household Solutions: 'Arrogant,' 'unresponsive,' 'inflexible,' 'unreliable in delivery,' 'unprofessional.'

"These same words are reflected by the consumers: 'Unresponsive,' 'don't care about the little guy,' 'arrogant . . .'" Seaborne paused. "You get the picture." Silence again filled the boardroom, but it was no longer the silence of skepticism. It was a blend of confusion and worry. "Anecdotal evidence supports this," she continued. "Did any of you know there was a website out there called www.householdsolutionssucks.com? Or that there are seven blogs dedicated to people who are frustrated with your company? Did you know that your distribution network—the buyers—get together over drinks to swap Household Solutions stories at trade shows? Do you follow the comments on Twitter?" A quick glance around the room told Seaborne that they didn't.

"So you see," she said quietly, looking first to Tetu, then to the rest of the group, "pricing isn't the issue. It's your customer service—or perhaps better said—your lack of it."

"Price does play a role, of course," she continued as Tetu prepared to object, "but not to as great an extent as you might believe. There is a great deal of research to support this. The studies all agree that, in virtually every industry, when given a choice between lower prices or better service, seventy-five to eighty percent of consumers will choose better service.

"In fact," Seaborne said with conviction, "as far as pricing strategies go, this is where the good news begins. Given the overwhelmingly positive attitudes consumers have toward your products, you might actually be better off *increasing* your prices. But that's only if—and it's a big if—you can turn around the way people feel about your company as a whole." On the two next screens Seaborne displayed a spreadsheet and line graph. "These are our projections for Household Solutions Inc. over the next five years. The first is if you maintain the same course you are on now. The second is a conservative estimate if you focus on improving your customer experience."

The numbers were impressive, and on the surface, believable. She stepped back from the screens, glanced at her watch, and said, "There's a lot more, of course, but Mr. Ogilvy was insistent on the time allotted to me—which is now up." She smiled for the first time since entering the room. "I'd like to thank you all," she concluded sincerely, "and wish you the best of luck with your journey."

At this, Gerard stood, turned to his team, and looked at Seaborne. "On behalf of all of us, Emily, I would like to thank you." He looked around at the silent faces. "I'm assuming that while there are many questions on details, there are none about the general context of this report?" Heads shook all around. "Great, then," he said. "A full copy was placed on each of your desks while we were in the meeting. You have all day today and tonight to read it through. We will reconvene here tomorrow morning for a one-hour meeting to share ideas. This is now everyone's top priority. Let's figure out where we go from here, shall we?"

Cameron sat for a moment collecting his thoughts while the others filed out of the room. Slowly he picked up his things and rose to leave. Gerard's voice came from across the table. "Where do you think you're going?" he asked. He was still seated, and looking at Cameron intently.

CHAPTER FIVE

CAMERON TURNED AND LOOKED at Gerard quizzically. "You did get the email about the extra half-hour, didn't you?" Gerard asked.

"Um, yes," Cameron replied, confused. He glanced out the door. "Do you want me to bring everyone back in?"

"Why would I want you to do that?" asked Gerard with a twinkle in his eye. He motioned to Cameron's chair. "Have a seat."

Cameron looked stupidly at it. *Was I the only one who was asked for the extra half-hour? Maybe I'm just dreaming,* Cameron thought hopefully. *Any moment I'll wake up, with a great night's sleep behind me and an exciting, predictable day in front of me.*

"Something on your mind, Cam?" Gerard's voice cut in.

Cameron quickly pulled the chair out and sat. "Not at all," he said in an unconvincing attempt to sound confident. "What's up?"

Gerard studied him for a long moment before he spoke. "How long have you been with the company, Cameron?" he asked. His eyes were fixed on Cameron's.

"Coming up to ten years, I guess," Cameron replied.

"You've done a heckuva job for us, you know." It was a statement, not a question. Cameron smiled modestly but said nothing. "I'm curious," Gerard continued after a long pause, "about what you thought of Ms. Seaborne's presentation." His gaze didn't shift from his vice president.

"Well," Cameron replied, "without having seen the details, her argument seems pretty solid. I mean, I'd really like her to be wrong, but I have a nagging suspicion she isn't."

Gerard nodded and looked at the now-blank LED screens. "Me too," he agreed. "And between me and you, I feel a little stupid we didn't see this ourselves. You'd think *someone* would have noticed and said, 'Hey, wait—where did our customers go?'" He turned back to Cameron. "So what do we do about it?"

Cameron blinked. *Why is he asking me?* "Aw, I'm just a simple engineer," Cameron said after a moment. "I'm probably not the right person to ask about customer service."

Gerard barked out a laugh, then leaned forward, eyes boring into Cameron's. "Wrong answer," he said. "Try again."

Cameron thought for a moment, then gave an apologetic shrug. "Off the top of my head, I've got nothing. To be honest, it's not even close to my area of expertise. And, well, don't get me wrong, but it's really not my department."

Gerard considered this for a moment. "So exactly whose department is it, then?" His steady gaze was starting to unnerve Cameron.

"I don't know," Cameron protested. "Sales, marketing, HR—one of those. But it certainly doesn't fall under product development or operations. I'm not trying to be difficult, really. I'm just not quite sure why you're asking *me*."

Gerard smiled. "Let me rephrase the question." He paused for a moment, put his fingertips together, and looked up at the ceiling. "Who is Household Solutions' CCXO—chief customer experience officer?"

Cameron narrowed his eyes warily, then shook his head. "We don't have one," he said. Gerard's face broke into a broad grin as his gaze returned to Cameron.

"Wrong answer again," he said.

It took a moment to take shape in Cameron's consciousness. "What? You're not thinking of me?" he pointed to himself with a confused look. Gerard just kept grinning.

"No . . . oh no . . . I mean, thanks and all, but . . . no . . . I do production and development . . . I can't just . . ." Cameron sputtered, completely at a loss for words. "What do I know about customer service?"

"Let me get this straight," Gerard said, interrupting Cameron's attempt to speak. "I'm offering you a jump all the way to corporate officer, with the salary and all the perks that go with it, and you're thinking of turning it down?" His grin got even wider, and he leaned even closer toward his tongue-tied employee.

"Grp," was all Cameron could get out.

"That's better!" Gerard said enthusiastically, standing and extending his hand to Cameron. "Welcome aboard!"

Cameron shook the hand weakly and nodded dumbly. *What just happened?*

"First things first," Gerard said as he walked around the table. "I'll have my assistant draft up the announcement to distribute to the employees tomorrow afternoon. We will, of course, announce it to the executive team when we meet in the morning. You're going to need a little time to get things organized, but unfortunately, we don't have that luxury. See me at two, and I'll walk you through what I want from you. Congratulations, Cam. I've got high expectations!" Gerard turned and strode away.

A promotion. He hadn't seen *that* coming. Cameron knew he should be thrilled; so why did he feel like he just jumped on a live hand-grenade?

CHAPTER SIX

AT TWO O'CLOCK, CAMERON MADE his way into Gerard's office. He had taken the time to collect his thoughts and do a little research. He wanted to have as much ammunition as he could. He'd thought about it, and there was no way he wanted the job. When he walked in, Gerard was bent over in his chair with his back to the door, rummaging through the bottom drawer of a filing cabinet.

"Hi, Cam," he said, without looking around. "Have a seat." Cameron sat. A moment passed, then Gerard gave a resigned sigh, and turned around in his chair. "Can't ever find something when you need it," he said, almost to himself. Looking up at Cameron, he smiled. "So, let's get started."

"About that," Cameron interjected. He had regained his composure since Gerard's surprise. "I've read the JMB report and totally agree on their recommended strategy." He shifted in his seat and continued, "I'm just not sure we need to appoint a chief customer experience officer to achieve it. It's a bit of overkill, isn't it? I mean, how hard can it be to make this adjustment? I'm not an expert on customer service, but I'm sure we can turn this around pretty quickly without going overboard."

Cameron continued. "Even if we did need someone dedicated to customer service, it probably doesn't have to be an officer, and I'm absolutely positive I'm not your guy for the job. Look, you've known me for a long time. When have I ever balked at a project or an opportunity? It's not me I'm worried about, it's the company. Sure, I'd love the promotion. But customer service just isn't my thing."

Gerard once again locked Cameron's eyes with his own, although the grin that had been on his face in the previous meeting did not reappear. His voice was serious and measured. "All right," he said, "objections noted. So let's examine your assertions one at a time." He leaned back in his chair with his hands on the desk in front of him. "In one sentence, what would you say was the essence of JMB's recommendation?"

Cameron thought for a moment. "That creating a distinguishable difference in customer service will give Household Solutions a competitive edge in the market."

"Good," Gerard replied. "Do you agree with it, based on the information they provided?"

"Yes," Cameron replied, "but . . ."

"Would it be fair to say that, in order to effectively execute this, it will have to happen at all levels of the company, beginning at the executive level?" Gerard continued, ignoring Cameron's objection.

"Of course," said Cameron, "but . . ."

"And that if we don't successfully implement it, the company is at serious risk?"

"It would seem so," Cameron said, a little exasperated, "but I . . ."

"So, if not a chief customer experience officer, with the power and authority to influence these changes throughout the workplace, how can we make sure they'll happen? Perhaps you're thinking I should just send a memo asking people to be nicer? Wave a wand and fix it? Just expect things to turn around on their own? Expect the other people in the company to accept a change in direction more easily than you're accepting this?"

Cameron fell silent.

"I believe in JMB's conclusions, Cameron," Gerard continued, "even though I don't want to. Imagine how hard it was for me to hear someone say about the company I founded and led for

25 years that 'your customers don't like you.' But the evidence is overwhelming. And the cost of continuing to have customers not liking us is too great."

"Do you know what our average Customer Lifetime Value is?" Gerard pressed Cameron.

Cameron nodded. It was burned into his brain. Household Solutions' CLV was a fairly complex equation that determined how much of the company's products a customer might buy over the course of a lifetime. Household Solutions focused on kitchen and household appliances and aids, and Cameron remembered being surprised at how many toasters, blenders, coffee makers and other items someone would purchase between the ages of 25 and 70.

"Okay," said Gerard. "And do you know roughly how many customers we have, based on our warranty database?"

Cameron nodded again.

Gerard pulled out his phone, opened up a calculator app, then slid it to Cameron. "So, let's do the math. Let's imagine that just one percent of our customers are getting annoyed with us, then stop purchasing our products. What is the potential impact on revenue?"

Cameron didn't need the calculator. If he nothing else, he was good at numbers. "Seven point two million dollars," he said.

It was Gerrard's turn to nod. "And that's not even taking into account the word-of-mouth factor, and the apparent issues with our distribution channel," he said. "My guess is that we could safely increase that number by a factor of five, wouldn't you?" Gerard was more intense now than Cameron had ever seen.

"Probably," Cameron said, doing the math in his head. "Probably more than that."

"That's *every year*," Gerard added, then took back the phone, tapped on it, and looked at the display. "So I'm thinking that trying to rebuild our reputation, save the company from failure, and recapturing a minimum of thirty-six million dollars *a year* in lost revenue is something I don't want left to chance."

"I agree," Cameron said. And he did. Gerard's argument was persuasive, if not a little frightening. "But all the more reason that I'm not your guy. If it's this important, why put someone with absolutely no expertise in charge? There are a lot of people in the company who know a lot more about customer service than I do. There are even more people outside of our company." He waved one arm in a big arc. "After all, there's no reason we can't bring in a hired gun."

"I thought of that," Gerard replied, "but I need someone to implement this at a senior level, and someone who knows our company and our business inside and out. If we need to find a hired gun to help us out, so be it. But I need someone with the sole responsibility and absolute authority to proactively drive this. I need someone who has the respect of the executive team, and I need someone I know I can trust implicitly." His eyes were back on Cameron. "You want to know why I chose you? I'll tell you."

Gerard took a sip from the water glass on his desk, careful to set it back down on its leather coaster. He turned his gaze to the window while he spoke. "I want someone who will come at this with fresh eyes and a fresh perspective. You're the best person on the team for that. It's not that I don't have confidence in the other senior management members—I do. You know how much I respect them. But the one thing that you can bring to the table they can't is that, by your own admission, you have no preconceived ideas as to how to approach customer service. You'll have to start from scratch. And in order for this company to be transformed, I think we may have to start from scratch in some ways. With the hill we have to climb, I don't think just 'good' customer service will cut it. We need *outstanding* customer service. We need to *wow* our customers.

"Cam, you're methodical and thorough in your approach, albeit sometimes a little resistant to change." Gerard turned back to Cameron, his grin reappearing. "You're the guy that can do this. Household Solutions needs you. I really need you. Are you in?"

Cameron thought a moment, looking across at Gerard. *Resistant to change? Me?* "Okay," he said finally, matching the CEO's gaze, "but I'll need more of that good coffee."

CHAPTER SEVEN

CAMERON'S CAR WAS STOPPED dead in traffic. His mind, however, was racing. He had accepted Gerard's challenge, and now he had to figure out how to get things moving. In their afternoon meeting, Gerard had outlined his plan to Cameron. Tomorrow morning, the senior executives would voice their thoughts. Cameron would consider each perspective, and then return Friday with his own recommendation to Gerard. From that point on, Cameron would be charged with researching and developing a strategic plan. Then he'd implement it throughout the company.

His newly created position gave him the authority to supersede any decision made in the company by anyone other than Gerard. This was necessary, Gerard had explained to him, to avoid inevitable squabbles as people adjusted to the changes. In some ways, it made him the second most powerful person in the company. Cameron wondered how the others would react.

For most of the fifty-five minute drive, Cameron tried to figure out the process for creating a customer-focused culture in the company. He wasn't quite sure where to begin. *What do we need to achieve? What should customer service at Household Solutions look like? What are we doing wrong? What, to use*

Gerard's terminology, was outstanding *customer service? What exactly was 'Wow'?*

He was still asking himself these questions as he pulled into his driveway. He listened as he walked toward the front door, then began counting down mentally when his foot hit the first wooden step of his front porch. *Three ... two ... one ...* An excited yelp came from the living room as Chewbacca heard leather on wood. Cameron reached the door and opened it in time to see a flash of blonde streak past him. This made Cameron happy. Sometimes Chewy made a grand exit. Sometimes he just hit the door. It was all in the timing.

An hour later, both he and dog walked and fed, Cameron punched the power button on his laptop and sat down in front of it. He typed "customer service" into the search engine: nearly five hundred million hits. *Yikes. This might take a little longer than I thought.* Cameron sat back and stared at the screen in silence.

Another idea occurred to him. He leaned forward, brought up the website for one of the big booksellers, and searched for customer service titles. Sixty-two thousand, eight hundred and ninety-seven. He fell back in his chair again and rubbed his temples. *Oh crap,* he thought. He looked over at the dog who was lying comfortably in front of the television. Chewy looked back at him. He had nothing, either.

CHAPTER EIGHT

CAMERON SAT AT HIS office the next morning in front of his computer, head buried in both hands. Another sleepless night, another early morning. Gerard's Blue Mountain coffee offered the only bright spot. He had carefully avoided the CEO this morning, afraid that his boss might ask him how things were going. Four hours of surfing the net had produced way too much information to process, including a mountain of trite drivel that had given him a pounding headache. This morning he had ordered no fewer than twelve books online—the ones that looked the most promising. Still, he felt no further ahead. He hoped the upcoming meeting might point him in the right direction.

He was ten minutes early and first to enter the meeting room. *Hey,* he thought with a wry grin as he looked at the table, *given my new position, maybe I should change seats.* But he opted against rocking the boat more. He wondered again how everyone else would react to his promotion. Yesterday he was on the lower tier of the senior management team. Today he was an equal to the CFO and COO. Actually, if you wanted to be technical about it, he was above them in the pecking order—at least in how Gerard defined the role. Cameron swallowed. *Am I ready for this?*

One by one, they started to arrive. Susan Tremmel carried with her a frighteningly tall stack of binders. It was a stark contrast to Stan Tetu, who had only a cup of coffee and a small flash drive. Gerard, who came in last, was emptyhanded. He didn't bother to sit down. "All right," he began without preamble, "who's first?"

Glances all around, until Gayle Humphries raised her hand and stood. "I might as well get the ball rolling," she began with a smile, reaching into her briefcase. The CFO extracted a small stack of paper and handed everyone a neatly typed, two-page document. "It's pretty high level, of course. Hard to reinvent the world in eighteen hours, but it's a start. Will and I worked on this together. I hope that was okay." She glanced at Gerard for approval. Gerard nodded.

"We focused on our distribution channel—the retailers and wholesalers who carry our products. We're thinking we can have tremendous success by introducing customer service on a sliding scale. We'll evaluate our clients and place them on one of four tiers based on size and profitability. Those clients who are on the top tier, the most profitable, will receive the highest service levels. The levels of service offerings will decrease as their importance to our company decreases. Those on the bottom will be provided a less intensive, more self-serve platform. In this way, the expense of providing higher service levels will be proportional to the profitability of the customer. This approach helps us reduce dissatisfaction with higher value customers, while at the same time managing the costs of delivering higher service levels."

Humphries spent another five minutes expanding on her concept. When she was done, and hands went up, Gerard rose and interrupted. "I suggest that we hear everyone out before we begin discussion. In fairness to all of you, no one has had adequate time to thoroughly process their ideas. So I think debate at this time might be a little premature." Hands went down, and everyone nodded in agreement.

"In fact," he continued, "let's restrict this morning to ideas only. We'll all share our thoughts today but leave discussion to a future meeting. This will give us all time to mull over each other's presentations." Nods again. Gerard sat back down.

The next to present was Susan Tremmel. She handed everyone two thick binders and stepped to a flip chart against the wall. "I think it's obvious that customer service is about people. And the better trained and developed our people are, the better our service levels will be."

"I put together a couple of things for us to use as a resource. In the blue binder," she indicated the thicker of the two, "is a description of the core competencies that surround customer service behaviors. I've taken these from a few different sources and indexed them to the broad employee categories we have at Household Solutions."

"The key is to build a competency map, and then do a gap analysis to determine each employee's current proficiency. From there, we will design a competency-based training structure—a Customer Service University, if you will—to bring everyone up to speed." Tremmel began going through the binder a page at a time to review the competencies. Cameron struggled to maintain focus as she explained the competency matrices appearing one after the other. *I am so in over my head,* he thought.

Ten minutes later, Tremmel was finished, her presentation gently but effectively hastened along by Gerard. Tetu stood next, walked to the computer, and inserted his flash drive. Instantly the company's website appeared on the center screen.

"We need to make it easier for people to do business with our company," he began, "from our website to our sales policies. Susan is right about training, I think. But we also have to make sure that the non-people side of our business is functioning properly."

"Take a look at this page, for instance" he pointed to the screen. "If you were a retailer or wholesaler trying to find your account status, where would you click first?" Cameron looked at the home page, larger than life on the monitor, and scanned the navigation bar. *Home, Products, About Household Solutions, Our History, Customer Care, Contact Us.* Below it, in smaller type was a second navigation bar, with *Coffee & Tea, Toasters & Ovens, Large Appliances, Irons & Laundry, Food Prep & Storage, Cooking.* Cameron scanned the promotional material in the body of the website. Nothing.

"It's not there!" Syd Rosen exclaimed. He looked incredulously at Tetu. "Is this right? I can't believe our commercial customers can't access their accounts!" Murmurs rippled around the table.

Realization came suddenly to Cameron. He pointed to the upper left of the screen. "Wait a minute. It's a trick! This is the consumer website. The site we use for our distribution channel is a different address."

Tetu waited for this to register with everyone, then hung his head in mock embarrassment. "You caught me," he said with a smile. "But even so, a huge number of our trade customers continually call us trying to find out how to access their account. Even though we have advertised and notified them about the commercial portal ad nauseam, they still go to the consumer one. What we really need is a small link that allows them to navigate to the right place. My point is, there are a lot of little things that make doing business with us a chore. Our Terms and Conditions, as another example, are a constant source of frustration for our sales team. We try to build up a strong relationship with customers, but when a customer is just ten days late with a payment, they're getting calls from accounts receivable. It's annoying, and customers complain about it all the time."

"Hang on just a second," Will Abbott turned to him. "Collecting receivables is just prudent business practice. That hardly falls under the category of poor customer service."

Gerard put his hand up and cut in before Tetu could respond. "Ideas only," he said to Abbott gently. "No discussion today, remember?" Abbott sat back begrudgingly, glaring at Tetu.

Syd Rosen was the next to stand up. He glanced around the room. "I think we have to differentiate ourselves from the competition," he said. His pronounced Brooklyn accent cut through the air with authority. "And the best way to do that is to improve our responsiveness." He began to slowly pace back and forth and spoke as if thinking aloud. He pointed at himself with both hands.

"I'm as guilty as everyone. The truth is, we have to be able to get the right products to our customers quickly and efficiently. For example, we've been functioning to date with the best just-in-time processes we could develop. But all too often, just-in-time turns into just-a-little-too-late." The COO looked at Cameron apologetically. "This isn't a reflection of you, Cam, it's our process. We need to start carrying larger inventories of our line so that we don't have to rely so much on forecasting. Backorders and delays create frustration and drive our customers to look for alternative suppliers. The more responsive we become, the better experience we will be able to provide." He stopped his pacing and sat down. "Sorry," he said to the group, "no fancy handouts or cool slideshows."

Only one presentation remained. All eyes turned to Cameron. He flushed with embarrassment as it dawned on him that everyone was expecting something from him, too. Before he could think of something to say, however, Gerard intervened. "Ah," he said loudly, with a big smile. He stood and looked at Cameron. "I knew I'd forgotten something."

The team looked at Gerard and back to Cameron quizzically. "I asked Cameron to just listen to your comments today, rather than participate," Gerard said matter-of-factly. "I thought it might give him a little inspiration for his new project." Curious glances bounced around the room. Cameron sat frozen, not sure what he was supposed to do.

"Ladies and gentlemen," Gerard said proudly, gesturing to Cameron, "I'm pleased to introduce Household Solutions new CCXO, chief customer experience officer. Cameron is officially in charge of transforming this company's culture to one focused on outstanding customer service. The perspectives you've provided today were excellent, and I'm sure have given him a great deal of insight. We needed a starting point, and now he's got it. To be successful, however, he'll need all the support and cooperation you can give him."

Cameron hadn't known what to expect from the group when the announcement was made, so he took the initial silence that greeted Gerard's proclamation in stride. Rosen was the first to speak. He pursed his lips into an expression of deliberation, then slowly nodded his head, looked down the table at Cameron with a smile and said, "Nice."

Humphries remained thoughtful and quiet, eying Cameron with unnerving steadiness.

Tremmel looked around the room, then spoke to Gerard. "Chief customer experience officer?" she asked skeptically. "I've never heard that title."

"Me neither," Gerard grinned. "You'll have to add a whole new category to that binder."

"But what will be his role in the company?" Tremmel persisted. "Who will report to him?" Good questions. Expectant eyes fell on Gerard.

"Cam's job is to define what a customer-focused version of Household Solutions should look like. Then he'll identify what needs to be done throughout the company to make it happen. An internal ombudsman of sorts, with a broad mandate to make things better."

"As to the question of who reports to him, right now we all do." Eyebrows raised in unison around the table. Gerard continued. "In order for this to work, he'll have to poke his nose into each of your silos and root around. Our jobs are to make sure he gets everything he needs to be successful." He paused for a moment to look into the faces of each team member. His tone left no room for doubt. "I've given him absolute authority to implement the changes he thinks need to be made. The only one who can overrule him is me—and I'd need pretty convincing evidence to do that.

"If you believe, as I do, the implications of what we heard yesterday, then you know this is possibly the most important initiative we've ever embarked on." His rich, baritone voice seemed to fill the room. "We need to change how we do things. There will be no time for egos, excuses, or turf wars. We, around this table, need to be absolutely focused, and we will need to work together as a team. Can I count on you?"

Heads nodded seriously around the room, but no one spoke. It was Rosen again who broke the silence. "So, what you're telling me is that I now report to Cameron," he said, looking at Gerard.

"In a manner of speaking, yes," Gerard confirmed.

Rosen looked at Cameron, then back at Gerard. "Well I for one think it's a great idea," he said, almost straight-faced. "He was a crappy employee. Who knows? Maybe he'll be a good boss."

CHAPTER NINE

CAMERON FOLLOWED GERARD BACK to his office after the meeting. "So," Gerard asked once they were seated, "what do you think?"

"That I'm totally the wrong person for this. Any one of them" he said, tipping his head toward the boardroom, would have been a better choice. They obviously have a much better handle on things. Graphs, charts, binders. All I could manage to bring to the table was a headache."

Gerard smiled and leaned forward to pick up the heavy blue binder from the meeting. He weighed it briefly in his hands. "Yep, there sure was a lot of stuff brought to the meeting." He set the binder down and looked at Cameron. "But I'm more interested in your observations about the meeting itself."

Cameron thought for a moment. "It would certainly appear," he said slowly, "that customer service can be interpreted in quite a few different ways. I was actually a little surprised that no two people had the same approach."

"Tell me more about that," Gerard said.

"Well," Cameron glanced at his notes, "Gayle seemed to be a proponent of a customer ranking approach for our distribution channel, with tiered service levels to balance cost with customer value. Susan's idea was a highly structured employee evaluation and training process. Stan thinks we should focus on accessibility, and Syd is suggesting we improve our responsiveness." He flipped his notebook shut, and looked up at Gerard. "And that was with less than 24 hours of prep time. Goodness knows what they'd come up with if you gave them a week! That's the thing, Gerard. I haven't even gotten out of the starting gate, and they're all a mile ahead of me."

Gerard sat back and studied Cameron for a moment. *"Oh wad some power the giftie gie us to see oursels as ithers see us,"* he said with a smile. "Robbie Burns. I guess it's probably unfair for me to expect you to see what I see." He leaned forward. "Look, Cam, each of their ideas had merit, I grant you. But each also had one giant flaw." Cameron looked quizzically at Gerard.

"Each of their ideas directly related to their own disciplines. Think about it. Gayle focused on the financial side, Susan on employees, Stan on marketing . . ."

"And Syd on operations," Cameron finished his sentence. "You're saying that each responded according to their own paradigm," he continued, now understanding where the CEO was leading him. "And we need to look at the company from a bigger perspective."

Cameron thought for a moment, then said, "Customer service might not even be the right way to describe the issue. It's the overall *customer experience*, with customer service being just one part of it." Gerard nodded in agreement.

"Which," Cameron continued, "makes the whole thing even further away from my area of expertise. And on top of that, what makes you think I'm going to be any more objective than everyone else?"

"Because I know my team," Gerard said plainly. "And just as I knew how the others would respond to my challenge from yesterday, I know that you will be the most objective." He grinned at Cameron. "You aren't happy until you have a complete understanding of things. You're like a dog with a bone when it comes to projects—you won't let go until you've nibbled around all sides and you know everything is just the way it should be."

Gerard glanced at his computer and chuckled. "Seems I'm

not the only one who feels that way. Here, let me show you something." Gerard spun his monitor around.

Gerry, I just wanted you to know I think your choice for this job is brilliant. I'll bet money he tries to turn this down, but don't let him. He's our best shot at this. The only downside is that you've left me scrambling for a replacement. The message was signed simply SR. Cameron blinked. It was from Syd Rosen, his boss up until a few minutes ago.

Gerard turned the monitor back and sat down. His voice softened as he continued. "Truthfully," he said to Cameron, "I don't really know the best approach, or whose perspectives will be the most useful to you. I really don't even know how difficult this project will be. But if you need additional people or external resources, go ahead and get what you need. Don't worry about waiting for formal approvals."

Cameron, deep in thought, nodded. "I'll need some time to wrap my head around everything," he said, "but hopefully in a few weeks I'll figure out what we're up against, what resources we might need, and what kind of timelines we might be looking at."

Gerard shook his head slowly. "My gut is telling me that time may not be on our side, Cameron. I think we need to act fast. Let's pull out all the stops on this. In fact . . ." He paused for a moment, then opened his top center desk drawer and rifled through it briefly. Unable to find what he was looking for, he scowled and went over to a high bank of file cabinets. After a minute of searching, he stopped and rubbed his upper lip with thumb and forefinger. In one stride he reached the telephone on his desk and punched the speed dial for his assistant. "You there, Charlize?" he said, not waiting for an answer.

"Uh, yes, Mr. Ogilvy?" came the voice over the speaker phone.

"Remember my friend told me about that person a while back. You know—the one who was supposed to be so good. Do you still have the information?"

"I think so. Let me just check."

Cameron couldn't help but smile. Those had to be the vaguest instructions he had ever heard. How Gerard's assistant was ever able to interpret "my friend who told me about a person a while back" was beyond him. But after just a few moments, her voice came through the speaker.

"Got it." Moments later, she breezed into the office holding a piece of paper with a name and phone number. "There was just a first name," the assistant said apologetically. "Is there anything else?"

Gerard shook his head and thanked her. He handed the note to Cameron and said, "Call this person. My friend says she's the best. Learn as much from her as you can."

Cameron looked down at the note. *Madeleine*, it said, along with a Los Angeles telephone number. "Thanks," he said to Gerard. "I'll let you know how it works out." He stood and started to leave, then turned back to Gerard. "Do I have a budget for this?" he asked, indicating the sheet of paper in his hand. "I mean, how much do we pay this consultant?"

The CEO shrugged. "No clue," he said. "But knowing my friend, he wouldn't have referred her if she wasn't the best in the business. Whatever she charges, I suspect she's worth it."

Cameron turned to leave, but Gerard stopped him. "Cam," he said. "I'm going to postpone next Monday's meeting to give you a little breathing room, but we need to see a plan sooner than later." Cameron nodded, picked up the note, and made his way out through the door and down the hall.

CHAPTER TEN

BACK IN HIS OWN OFFICE, Cameron dialed the number on the note. After three rings, a cheerful voice came on: "Hello! This is Maddy. Sorry I missed you. I've probably forgotten to turn my phone on again. Leave a message—but make sure it's interesting, or I might forget to call you back!"

Cameron hesitated briefly. "Hi. It's Cameron Whitehall from Household Solutions. I was given your name, and I was hoping to discuss with you a customer experience project we're working on." He recited his direct phone line, then hung up. *Here's hoping she's as good as advertised,* Cameron thought to himself.

There was no returned call by six o'clock, so Cameron decided to head home. He'd tried the number a few more times and spent an hour on his computer searching for customer service consultants. The fifty-nine million hits daunted him at first, but after a quick scan he realized most referred to call center agents and retail sales clerks. A search of customer experience consultants gave him mostly large, important-sounding management consulting companies that didn't really specialize in customer experience, and customer service training companies that didn't seem to have the strategic expertise he was looking for. No one jumped out at him. He couldn't find anyone named Madeleine anywhere.

That evening, Cameron sat on the leather couch in the living room with his attention equally divided between the television, the traffic going by the front bay window, and Chewbacca's intense scrutiny of an invisible creature just out of reach in the corner of the room. On a whim, he reached for his cell phone and punched in the consultant's number, which he'd already memorized. *How sad is that?*

"This is Maddy!" came the cheerful reply halfway through the second ring.

"Um, hi," Cameron began. "My name is Cameron Whitehall. I'm with Household Solutions, and I was . . ."

"I *LOVE* Household Solutions!" her excited voice interrupted. "I must own *everything* you've ever made. My favorite is the *Va-Pure Lock* containers—you know the ones with the little device on the side to pump the air out so food will stay fresher? They are GENIUS!" Cameron knew them well. They were his design. "And the *Vertical Drop* toaster—I love that one too," she continued before Cameron could say anything. "You know the one where the toast slides down onto a tray when it's done? No more of that annoying buzzing sound when it doesn't pop properly. And the *SlimFridge* and the *Single Serving* dishwasher, and the . . ." Cameron listened in amazement as the woman on the other end of the phone listed off a dozen of their products.

"So are you calling about the letter I sent in last October about how hard it is to get replacement parts for the rechargeable Counter Scrubber?" she asked.

Cameron wasn't quite sure what to say. "Um, actually I, um . . ." he began.

"I'm just joking," the voice interrupted with a bubbling laugh. "Ralph, I think he's a friend of Household Solutions' big boss, told me you'd be calling. Besides, I know better than to expect a response to my letter from Household Solutions. Would you like to get together Monday?"

Cameron held the phone out in front of him and stared at it for a moment. Bringing it back over his ear, he said uncertainly, "Sure. How about nine, my office?"

"Oh, gee," Madeleine said disappointedly, "that's kind of a bad time. The stores open at nine." Then her tone brightened again. "No, wait—okay—nine o'clock. Meet me at CappuGino's in Beverley Hills. There's a hat shop there that I've been meaning to go to, and it doesn't open until ten. That will give us an hour."

"Um, sure," Cameron said. "I wouldn't want to stand in the way of your shopping."

"That's for sure!" Madeleine said earnestly. "See you at nine!"

Cameron stared dumbly at the phone. He looked over at Chewy who, having given up on his invisible friend, was now watching television. Cameron couldn't remember a stranger week. Now it looked like the next one would pick up where this one left off. *What kind of a consultant has to squeeze in work around shopping?* he thought. It was more than just unprofessional. It was . . . odd. Hanging up the phone, he resolved to try to go with the flow. *What was it Gerard had said? Resistant to change? Ha!* He'd show him.

He had no way of knowing, of course, that this was just the beginning.

CHAPTER ELEVEN

ON MONDAY AT 9:00, Cameron was waiting under a multi-colored umbrella at CappuGino's. The trip to Beverly Hills had added an extra half hour to his morning drive. Still, he'd left early and made it with almost thirty minutes to spare. He scanned the morning crowds for someone who looked like a consultant. He had no idea how to recognize Madeleine. He couldn't even guess her age. She talked like a sixteen-year-old cheerleader, but the timbre of her voice suggested someone much older.

Cameron was surprised to see so many people milling about on a Monday morning. He watched a young couple smiling and pointing at two living mannequins in one of the shop windows. A businessman strode by, talking loudly into his Bluetooth and gesturing wildly with both hands. He looked to Cameron like a well-dressed version of the homeless who wandered LA's eclectic downtown.

Cameron smiled as a flamboyant seventy-something woman walked briskly along the sidewalk. She wore a red and white blazer and skirt and a royal blue top. A red hat the size of a sombrero and fixed with a jaunty white flower perched on her black-and-white streaked hair. Her oversized, rhinestone-encrusted, white glasses would have made Lady Gaga proud. She looked like a caricature Miss America on medication.

As she walked by him, the woman's eyes focused sharply over Cameron's right shoulder. They widened and a bright smile spread across her face. She picked up steam and made a tight right turn into the restaurant. "Gino!" she shouted at some unseen individual, "where have you BEEN? It's been WAY too long!"

A sinking feeling instantly hit Cameron's stomach. He recognized the voice from his telephone conversation Friday night. *Really?* he thought. *Are you kidding me?* Moments later, hat and all, Madeleine stepped out of the restaurant and joined him.

Without introduction, she plopped herself into the chair opposite Cameron and said enthusiastically, "I LOVE this place! Ever since Gino started opening up his other restaurants, I just don't get to see him so much anymore. He makes the best cappuccino in the state!" She leaned toward Cameron conspiratorially, with her eyes looking first left, then right. "He's also *gorgeous*," she said with a wink.

Before Cameron could respond, the woman leaned back abruptly. Her face suddenly turned serious. She cocked her head. "Now, then. How may I help you?"

For the first time that he could remember, Cameron was quite literally speechless. His mouth opened, and no sound came out. The words from Mary Poppins flashed into his mind. *Close your mouth please, Michael, we are not a codfish.* But he couldn't help himself.

"Oh dear," the woman said, flushing as she saw Cameron's look of consternation. She scanned the restaurant. "This IS embarrassing!" she said as she began to rise. "I thought you were a Cameron Whitehall. I was supposed to meet him here, and I just didn't see anyone else. I just assumed . . ."

"I . . . I'm Cameron," Cameron tried desperately not to stutter. "Sorry, I just wasn't expecting . . . I mean, I was looking for . . ."

"Oh good!" she interrupted happily with an exaggerated sigh of relief, plopping back in her chair. Looking around again, she stage-whispered, "And don't worry, I understand. I'm tongue-tied on Monday mornings, too. Sometimes the brain just takes a bit to wake up." She looked up and waved to Gino, who had appeared beside them. "Two double-chocolate mochaccinos, please, Gino," she instructed pleasantly. "And I think you may want to make Mr. Whitehall's here with double espresso."

Cameron looked at Gino helplessly. *I guess I'm having a double-chocolate mochacccino,* he thought. Gino looked at the woman and bowed with a great flourish. "Your wish is my command, madam." Turning to Cameron with a quick glance back, he flashed a knowing grin, and said, "Take the double espresso. You'll be needing it."

As Gino disappeared back into the restaurant, the woman turned again to Cameron. "So, how can I help you, Cameron?" she asked pleasantly.

"Well, Madeleine," Cameron said, not exactly sure where to start, or how this eccentric old woman was really going to help, "Household Solutions is looking to change its culture to deliver outstanding, or 'wow,' customer experiences. I've been given the task of getting us there, and I was told you might be of assistance."

"How very flattering," Madeleine said with a smile. "By the way, call me Maddy. I find Madeleine far too hard to spell, don't you?" She reached up to adjust her hat. "But I'm curious why you feel you need *my* help. A big company like Household Solutions must have plenty of people who understand customer experience."

"No doubt," Cameron answered wryly, thinking back to the last senior management team meeting. "But I'm the one they've put in charge, and I'm pretty much out of my league. I need someone who can point me in the right direction in fairly short order. Can you help?"

Before Madeleine could answer, Gino reappeared with a tray and their two drinks. "Your mochaccino, madam," he said to Madeleine with a gracious smile and a flourish, "with chocolate shavings just the way you like it." Turning, he placed a gigantic mug in front of Cameron and gave him a sympathetic smile. "It's a triple," he said. "Five or six more of these, and you might just be able to keep up with her."

Cameron smiled back and thanked him, and Gino turned again to Madeleine. "I have not had the opportunity to tell you," he said with earnest, "how grateful I am for your suggestions. They have made a world of difference to my humble little cafés. For you, my beautiful lady, coffee is on the house forever."

"Why, thank you, Gino," Madeleine said, obviously touched by his sincerity. "The pleasure was mine. By the way, how many humble little cafés do you have now?"

"One hundred and ninety-three." He was unable to hold back the pride in his voice. "But I do as you say, and work outside here an hour a week. You were right. It keeps me grounded." He gently bowed to them, then excused himself to attend to a new table of customers. Madeleine watched Gino go with a smile, then turned back to Cameron. "So tell me more about Household Solutions and customer experience," she said.

Cameron told her in detail about the meeting with Emily Seaborne, and why they felt that improving their customer experience was so important. "Even though I've been given this responsibility," he said honestly, "I'm really just an engineer who normally focuses on product design and manufacturing. I mean, I think I recognize good experiences when I have them, but I'm not sure I understand it well enough to do what needs to be done here."

Madeleine regarded him again for a moment. As she did, Cameron noticed for the first time the bright blueness of her eyes. He had often read in books about people whose eyes danced and sparkled, but this was the first time he had actually seen it. "So, you've had a week to learn about customer experience," she said finally. "What have you learned so far?"

"Well," he said, recalling his discussion with Gerard, "I learned that there are a lot of different aspects to customer experience, and that people's perspectives differ greatly. I've discovered that it's a lot more complex than I originally thought." The expression on Madeleine's face stopped him for a moment.

"Oh, pish," she said dismissively. "What else?"

Cameron told her about his online research and the dozen books he had ordered. "Oh, books!" her face lit up. "I like books! Who wrote them?" Cameron told her. Madeleine shook her head, not recognizing any of the names. "What do these people do?" she asked. "What made you think they might be worth reading?"

"I don't know," Cameron began. "Looked like a few consultants and some academics. One, I know, was written by the former CEO of a well-known company."

Madeleine frowned. "Pity," she said with disappointment. Cameron looked at her questioningly. "Well, it seems to me," she continued, "that you're getting every perspective except the most important one."

"What's that?" Cameron asked, his interest stirring. Madeleine was about to answer, then glanced at her watch. "Heavens!" she suddenly leaped up and began adjusting her skirt. "It's almost ten o'clock! I'm late!" She put on a pair of gloves Cameron hadn't noticed before, smiled brightly at him, and placed a half-crumpled piece of note paper on the table. "Cameron," she said, "I know just what to do!"

She then made a little finger wave, turned, and began walking purposefully away. "Meet me tomorrow at nine-thirty," she said over her shoulder. "The address is on that piece of paper!" As she turned the corner she thrust her forefinger in the air and made a circular motion. "When the going gets tough, the tough go shopping!" she said, disappearing from sight.

Cameron glanced at the piece of paper, then at the now-empty chair in front of him. He blinked. *What just happened?* he asked himself for the second time in as many weeks.

Later that afternoon, back in his office, Cameron took a moment to look at the address. It was on a street just adjacent to the Santee Alley area—an eclectic, eccentric shopping district a few blocks north of the Santa Monica Freeway. Santee Alley was known as the place to go in Los Angeles for people in the market for cheap, knock-off designer goods. Cameron had bought a Rolex watch there once. It cost him $50 and lasted all of two weeks.

It seems an odd place for an office, Cameron thought, yet somehow appropriate for the odd woman. After their meeting, he had considered asking Gerard to double-check the reference, but decided against it. He'd already been too negative in his approach to this new position, and now that he had accepted the job, he wanted to be as proactive as possible. Besides, peculiar as she was, Cameron had an inexplicably positive feeling. He didn't know what it was, but his spidey-sense was definitely tingling.

He wasn't going to stop checking out other sources, of course, but he'd see how far this Maddy person would take him.

He'd realized after their morning meeting he'd neglected to talk business. *What were her rates? Did she have a contract for him?* He hadn't even been specific about her deliverables. He vowed to be better prepared for tomorrow's meeting, and set to work getting things organized.

CHAPTER TWELVE

THE DRIVE FROM HIS home to Santee Alley the next morning took Cameron only marginally longer than it did to find a parking spot. After circling several times, he finally spotted one in a parking garage on East Olympic Boulevard several blocks from his destination. With fifteen minutes to spare, he wheeled in, grabbed his portfolio, and jumped out of the car.

Walking briskly down the street, dodging around the early morning pedestrian traffic, he followed the numbers until he reached the one Madeleine had given him. He looked up at the inauspicious, four-story, stone building with full-length, multi-paned glass running along its length. It looked like a converted old manufacturing facility. On either side of the entrance were canopies protecting the street vendors from the elements. A single step led to a set of two solid, black, wrought-iron doors. Above them was a one-foot-high by three-foot-wide black marble plaque etched in *Saggezza Center*.

As Cameron approached the doors, it occurred to him he hadn't gotten a floor or suite number from Madeleine. *Oh well. Hopefully there will be a directory inside.* Then he realized he had no idea how she'd be listed. He groaned inwardly. *Great start to the morning,* he thought.

When he walked through the doors, he found himself in an immense, bare foyer. Thirty feet in front of him stood a long wall of glass doors revealing what appeared to be a large, dimly lit department store. To his left was a plain white wall with benches and non-descript doors. To his right were two banks of unmoving escalators and a black and white sign that read, "Welcome to Saggezza Center. Hours: 9:30am—10:00pm."

He walked to one of the benches on the wall and sat, wondering what to do next. He flipped opened his portfolio and checked the piece of paper Madeleine had given him. He was in the right place. Maybe she'd written down the wrong number. He pulled his cell phone out of his suit pocket, thought for a moment, then tapped in Madeleine's number. After three rings, the familiar voice message came on, *"This is Maddy. Sorry I missed you. I've probably forgotten to turn my phone on again . . ."*

Cameron jammed his phone back in his pocket, closed the portfolio, and slowly stood. No point in just waiting here hoping for divine intervention, he thought. He started toward the exit, and was halfway there when the lights in the department store blazed on. At the same time there was a reverberating clicking sound as the automatic locks on the store doors disengaged. Cameron glanced at his watch. Nine-thirty on the nose. As if on cue, the two iron entrance doors swung open, and he watched as women, men, and families began streaming through the foyer and into the store. Shoppers looking to get a head start on the day.

He waited for a surprisingly large number of incoming shoppers to slow before he attempted to exit. Two minutes later, though, the traffic showed no signs of abatement. Cameron's brow wrinkled in confusion. *Where are all these people coming from? They weren't standing outside just five minutes ago. How do they even know about this place?* Cameron had lived in LA all of his life, and this was the first time he'd ever heard of a Saggezza Center. He pulled his phone out and typed the name into a search engine. Nothing.

He glanced up at the crowd and saw the top of a lime green hat adorned with a large white feather moving toward him. He felt a small wave of relief. He was pretty sure he knew who it was.

As Madeleine came into view, he saw that her hat was accessorizing a conspicuous white and orange pantsuit with a fat, sixties-style belt. She stood out in a loosely tied paisley scarf that finished off the ensemble.

She spied him instantly as she entered, and a wide smile spread across her face. "Hello, Cameron!" she exclaimed, as if greeting a long-lost friend. "I am SO sorry to have kept you waiting! I always forget what rush hour is like in here." She looked at the seemingly unending river of incoming shoppers, and then back at Cameron. "Are you ready?" she asked.

"Absolutely," Cameron said with a smile, glancing around. "Where's your office?"

"Office?" Madeleine looked at him with amusement. "You are TOO cute! Come. Follow me." She turned and strode briskly toward the nearest of the two plain doors on the left side of the foyer. Cameron blinked, then hastened to catch up.

Through the doors was a small beige room with a lone set of elevator doors. Madeleine tapped a card on a scanner beside the doors, and the elevator opened. She walked in and Cameron followed. The elevator looked ancient, though the inside was much larger and more elegant than it appeared on the outside. The pecan finish and polished chrome reflected brightly off the mirrored walls. Madeleine reached for the control panel and pressed the lower-most black button. Etched into the brass plate beside the button was the letter 'B.' *Basement,* Cameron thought. The rest of the buttons read One, Two, Three, and . . . MOM.

Mom?

Moments later, the doors opened, and Cameron's eyes fell on what could only be described as a retail madhouse. Jammed with shelves, products, and shoppers, the first impression of the store was that a tornado had hit and people were combing through the rubble. Merchandise was stacked and strewn, and it seemed there was as much on the floor as on the shelves. The sheer randomness of things jarred Cameron's senses. He stood in the elevator looking out at the scene, trying to get oriented, until Madeleine took his hand and led him out and into the chaos.

"Where exactly are we going?" he asked, stepping over some packages of Tupperware. Madeleine stopped and looked at him.

She cocked a hip and flipped both hands outward to indicate the obviousness of where they were.

"Store," she said in a valley girl tone, as if it was the stupidest question ever. "Shopping." Then she smiled brightly at him, turned, and resumed her march through the maze of aisles. Cameron rubbed his eyes and followed dutifully behind.

"Shopping?" he asked as he caught up to her, then tripped over a bag of birdseed jutting out from a shelf. "I thought you were going to help us with our customer experience. Can you not wait and do your shopping after we're done?"

Madeleine stopped and spun abruptly, causing Cameron to almost collide with her. She looked straight at him. "There's a sale on sheets," she said matter-of-factly. "One hundred percent Egyptian cotton. Percale. Three hundred thread count. Half-price." She wheeled again and continued walking. "Egyptian cotton has the longest fiber and is known as the king of sheets," she said over her shoulder. "It actually gets softer and more comfortable every time you wash it."

Cameron again caught up to her and looked at her intense expression. "Oh. Well then, we wouldn't want to miss *that*."

"My point exactly," said Madeleine cheerfully, accelerating slightly.

They came to what seemed to pass for a bedding section, and Cameron stopped dead in his tracks. In front of him was a crush of shoppers surrounding what he assumed was the sale-priced sheets. It looked like an eight-person deep rugby scrum, with more people diving in by the minute. Madeleine carefully removed her hat and passed it to Cameron. "Would you be a darling and hold this for me?" she smiled. "If I'm not back in an hour, call for help!"

With elbows out, she waded into the crowd. Cameron watched with amazement as she was swallowed by the swarming shoppers. Occasionally, he caught a glimpse of her short, spiked, copper-colored hair bobbing and weaving somewhere in the middle. *Wait a minute,* he thought. *Copper? Wasn't it black and white yesterday?*

Three minutes later, she squirted out of the far side and wound her way back to Cameron, carrying two large bundles.

"Look at this!" she proclaimed excitedly. "*Four hundred* thread count. One California king flat, one fitted, and two king pillow cases! I was originally only going to buy the white, but at this price, I might as well get the blue as well, don't you think?" Before Cameron could answer, she thrust the sheets into his arms and retrieved her hat. Carefully arranging it back on her head, she said. "Now then. To work, shall we?"

She led Cameron up one of the main isles to the front of the store. There, he could see the escalators, now functioning and full of people. Madeleine stopped and turned. Cameron followed suit. With a regal sweep of her arm, she gestured at the store. "Okay. Tell me what you see," she demanded.

Cameron struggled to look over the bundles he held in his arms. "A department store?" he said simply. He looked at Madeleine. She was just glaring at him. "What?" he said defensively. "It's a department store. A little disheveled, I'll grant you, but that's what it is."

Madeleine heaved a sigh. "You don't shop much, do you?" she said.

"Of course I shop," Cameron replied. "Everyone shops. I get groceries once a week, clothes, things for my dog, stuff for my car. I shop as much as the next guy."

"Pish," Madeleine said dismissively. "That's not shopping. That's *buying*. Now look out again and tell me what you see."

Still unsure what to look for, Cameron slowly surveyed the store, his gaze sweeping from left to right. "The first thing that comes to mind is . . . chaos," he said. "I can't think of another word for it."

"Good," Madeleine nodded with approval, "that's a start. But here's the important question. What is it about the store that's making it appear chaotic?"

Cameron thought about this as he scanned the store. Before he could answer, Madeleine's eyes opened wide. "Oh my God!" she gasped with sudden realization, "I just remembered they were having a sale on 125-piece tool kits! Forty-piece, drop-forged socket set, seven screwdrivers, four pliers, three nut drivers, a tap and drill set, pry bar, level, hacksaw, meter . . ." She grasped his collar with both hands and looked into his eyes with excitement. "In a heavy-duty case. Regularly four hundred and ninety-nine dollars, now just two hundred fifty!"

Before Cameron could respond, she removed her hat again and set it on top of the two bedding sets in his arms. "Look around," she instructed, already turning to go. "Meet me in housewares in thirty minutes!" And with that, she power-walked away. Cameron watched her go. He shifted his gaze to the portfolio, bedding, and hat in his arms, then looked out at the store, then up at the ceiling. He was beginning to feel like he was in a dream again. Or maybe he was just being set up. He looked around in vain for hidden cameras. Sighing, he refocused on the store in front of him.

Slowly, he began to segment and categorize the things he was seeing. He walked down one of the narrow center aisles, his eyes scanning back and forth, and his brain sorting through the information. He turned and walked down another aisle, and began to see patterns—just with different merchandise. He wanted to make notes, but the load in his arms prevented this, so he concentrated on the key things to remember.

After twenty-five minutes, he began his search for the housewares section. It took him longer to find it than he had anticipated. To his surprise, the store was much larger than it appeared on the outside. He had been to London's Harrod's, and New York's Macy's, and this would easily rival them in size. He was also slowed by the absence of signage to point him in the right direction. He eventually found her, though, waiting with a large and heavy-looking plastic suitcase.

"Got the last one!" she said proudly as she plucked her hat from the top of Cameron's load. She then proceeded to wedge the suitcase handle into the fingers of Cameron's right hand and use both hands to arrange her hat. Cameron grimaced as he grasped the heavy suitcase.

Who needs this many tools? he thought.

He was expecting Madeleine to take the toolkit back from him, but instead she just turned and looked at him with a smile. "So," she said, "tell me what you've seen so far." Cameron shifted a little to get a better grip on his load and began to recite his observations.

"Well, first of all," he said pointedly, nodding to his full arms, "If they have shopping carts, they're well-hidden." Madeleine smiled sympathetically, but to his dismay didn't offer to take anything. "It seems to me," he continued, "that the chaos is due to a bunch of general things that have been neglected by the store. The result is that they really haven't made it easy to do business with them." As he said it, he realized that he was reciting Stan Tetu's words from just a few days before.

"How so?" asked Madeleine.

"Well," Cameron answered, "I'm not a retail expert, but to begin with, there's no discernable order to the merchandising. Yes, things are broken into broad categories, like housewares." He made a circular motion with his head to indicate their current location. "But other than that, everything seems pretty random. I walked through their pharmacy section, and saw toothbrushes on four different shelves. The placement of the products doesn't seem to follow any intuitive guide. It just looks like someone found a hole on a shelf and placed it there.

"The shelves themselves are too high," Cameron continued. "Even if they had made an effort to put the more common items within arm's reach it would be better, but they didn't. The aisles are very narrow, which is particularly a problem because of all the boxes and merchandise strewn all over the place. I felt like I was on a slalom course.

"As for the merchandise, only about half of it is priced. It looks like they've put pricing on shelves some of the time, but the stuff that is supposed to be on that shelf is somewhere else. How are people supposed to buy things when they don't know how much they cost? Some of the products had been taken out of the boxes and not put back in. Some of the things they do have on the shelves are just . . . bizarre. In sporting goods, for example, I saw a sixteen-foot section filled with hockey sticks. How many hockey sticks do we need in LA in April? I looked for baseball gloves, on the other hand, but couldn't find a single one."

Cameron paused for a moment, trying to recall the other things he had seen. His arms were starting to ache. "Like I said," he continued, "it's chaos. The floor is filthy, lights in entire sections are burned out, product merchandising is a shambles, they don't seem to have the right mix . . .

"Oh!" he exclaimed, as a memory flashed into his head. "And all over the store is Christmas signage. *Christmas.* It's April! You'd think they might get around to taking it down. It just seems like everything is a disaster. I can't even figure out how they're still in business."

Madeleine smiled at him. "Good start," she said approvingly. "You've missed the important things, of course, but nevertheless, it's a good start." She adjusted her hat. "Let's get out of here and have a coffee, shall we? I really have a craving for a large, iced raspberry cappuccino with organic light whipped cream and watermelon flakes on top."

Cameron nodded and followed Madeleine as she navigated them back through the aisles. *Missed the important things?* he thought. *What did I miss?*

Moments later, they reached the checkout area. Stretched in front of them were ten counters. Nine were new, automated, self-serve counters—the kind that require customers to scan their own merchandise. The last one had a lone, disinterested-looking cashier and a line of over thirty people.

Cameron groaned as his companion walked straight to the long line. His arms felt like lead. He awkwardly shifted the toolkit from one hand to the other. "Why don't we just use the self-serve counters?" he asked Madeleine. She just motioned for him to take a closer look at the self-serve areas.

In front of each self-serve counter was a sign. *If you're having difficulties, ask one of our customer service representatives for help.* Cameron watched as customers approached a counter and unsuccessfully tried to scan their goods. They craned their heads, looking for a customer service representative. After a minute or so of searching in vain, they gave up and made their way into the ever-increasing line for the single live cashier. The scene repeated itself, customer after customer, with eerie similarity.

"Do the automated checkouts not work at all?" Cameron asked Madeleine.

"I've never seen one work in here," she replied. "That's why I always go directly to the cashier."

Cameron shook his head in astonishment. "Why don't they

fix them?" he asked her. "Or at least have customer service people in place like the signs suggest? Why don't they put in more live cashiers?!"

"Good questions," Madeleine agreed, eyeing a rack with Chinese tea sets on sale. Cameron waited for her to elaborate.

After a moment, he turned to her and said, "You said that I'd missed the important things. What did I miss?"

Madeleine gaze's was still on the tea sets. "Another good question," she said, glancing briefly at him. Cameron waited again, but the eccentric woman said nothing.

"Thanks," he said, not attempting to hide his sarcasm. "That makes it much clearer."

"Do I have to tell you everything?" Madeleine said, turning, the twinkle returning to her eyes.

Cameron flushed. "Actually, it would be nice if you would tell me *something*. It is, after all, what I'm paying you for. Which reminds me," he said, suddenly thinking of the notes in the portfolio buried under the small mountain of merchandise in his arms, "what am I paying you?"

Again came the *what-a-stupid-question* look. "You're concerned about the oddest things," Madeleine laughed, then turned and walked toward the tea sets.

What the heck am I doing here? he thought. He watched Madeleine fussing with the stacks of tea sets. She selected one, held the box up, and squinted as if trying to imagine what it would look like in a dining room. After a moment, she picked up another one and did the same thing. Sighing, Cameron turned back to see how much the line had moved.

Cameron had first counted thirty-three people in front of them. There were now twenty-seven. The cashier was moving at glacial speed. Cameron did a double-take at the front of the line. Weren't those the same customers she was ringing through when he first got there? He squinted. It was. He recounted the people in line, and again came to twenty-seven. Where had all the other people gone?

Cameron watched curiously as the cashier dragged another item over the counter scanner. She peered at the display, frowned, and dragged it across again. Sighing, she brought the item slowly to her face, and began keying the numbers into the computer with one finger. She waited to see if it registered. It didn't. Picking up the item again, she poked some more at the keyboard. Suddenly, a middle-aged woman, about ten people in front of him, left the lineup. She looked around, then set a blender and two pairs of pants on a half-empty shelf and walked away. A minute later, a young man holding a new pair of Oakley sunglasses did the same. The line was now at twenty-five.

How does this place stay in business? Cameron thought again to himself. That was about four hundred dollars in lost sales with those two people alone. *This has to be the worst-run retailer in the whole city.* He looked behind him at the lineup, now at about forty people, and then at the self-serve cashes. He watched as person after person tried, looked for help, tried again, then gave up. At least a third of them took one look at the line, then set their products down and walked away.

One man, who looked to be in his late seventies, was getting increasingly frustrated with one of the self-serve machines. He looked at it with open hostility, and finally he waved his hand in disgusted resignation. He did some mental math, then placed some money down on the counter in front of him and walked through with three pairs of socks and a cordless sander. No sooner did he cross the threshold of the store, though, red lights began to flash, and two burly security people appeared from nowhere to brusquely usher him away. As the man was escorted through a non-descript door, angry and shouting, Cameron shook his head.

Madeleine returned just at that moment and lifted a robin's egg blue and peach tea set on top of Cameron's pile. The line was now only about ten people deep. Madeleine looked at Cameron, and then at his arms, which now were throbbing. "Oh, you POOR boy!" she exclaimed with sudden realization. "You must be exhausted!"

Cameron nodded wearily. "It is getting a little heavy," he admitted. *Understatement of the century,* he thought.

"Let me go find you a cart," Madeleine said firmly. "I'll be right back." And once again, she turned and walked away, this time toward the door that led to the small elevator room.

Cameron shifted to redistribute the load a little and waited. The two customers behind him were having an animated conversation about how much they hated shopping here—how there were never enough employees, and how hard it was to find things. If it weren't for the occasional bargain, and some things they couldn't get elsewhere, they both agreed they would never shop here again.

As he watched more closely, Cameron came to the conclusion that there weren't nearly as many customers in the store as he had originally thought. Most of the aisles he could see from his vantage point were empty, and the line was long because it was the only one available. The occasional crowd gathered around the deeply discounted merchandise—as he had witnessed with the sheet sets—but it would quickly disperse, with the bargain-hungry shoppers heading straight to the checkout.

Twelve minutes later, Cameron was finally at the cash, and the disinterested cashier began slowly sliding the items back and forth over the scanner. She didn't look up. She hadn't even acknowledged Cameron's presence. *An automaton,* Cameron thought. *No,* he thought again. *A zombie. Just like in the movies.* "Pretty busy in here today," he said cheerfully, hoping to brighten her mood.

She just looked up at him with blank eyes. "Six forty-three twenty-nine."

Cameron suddenly realized Madeleine hadn't returned with the cart or, more importantly, to pay for her merchandise. He looked around in vain. She was nowhere in sight. "Six forty-three twenty-nine," the cashier repeated, this time a little louder. Cameron looked at her and thought about explaining the situation, but the dead eyes told him it would be of no use. Sighing, he reached into his jacket pocket and extracted a credit card from his wallet. The cashier processed it in slow-motion and wordlessly handed him the slip. He took it, slid it into his wallet, and grunted as he again picked up the load.

"Here, let me take these from you!" Madeleine had suddenly appeared beside him with a large shopping cart. Cameron looked at her, then at the shopping cart. *Where on earth did she find it?* he wondered. He hadn't seen any others in the store. Smiling happily, Madeleine plucked the items from his arms one at a time and placed them carefully in the cart. "Goodness!" she said appreciatively, "These are *heavy!*"

Cameron began pushing his cart toward the elevator and turned for one last look at the store. The lone cashier walked away from her post. She had left a little sign on the conveyor belt at the cash that read, "On break. Back in 15 minutes." A collective groan rose from the line, and seven people set their merchandise on the floor and walked away. Cameron stared in astonishment.

"Shall we?" Madeleine's voice cut through his thoughts. With a big smile, she turned and walked briskly to the elevator door. Cameron trailed behind dutifully. "It looks like I'm going to have to pass on that iced raspberry cappuccino," Madeleine said apologetically as she pushed the elevator button. "I had completely forgotten about my nail appointment across town. So shall we meet here tomorrow morning—same time?"

Cameron looked at her uncertainly. "I'm not quite sure what more there will be to see here. I mean, it's a great example of a poorly-run company, for sure, but their issues seem to be more operational than experience-related."

Madeleine looked at him thoughtfully. "Well," she began slowly, "you're partially right, I suppose. But I think you might have it backwards. Didn't we go through this earlier?"

Cameron wrinkled his brow as he thought back. He had no recollection of having had that discussion. Madeleine patted him on the chest sympathetically. "You'll be fine," she said confidently. The elevator doors opened with a soft ding. "So, same time tomorrow?" she asked again.

"Um, sure," Cameron said as they entered the elevator. He glanced at his portfolio, finally now the only item in his hands. "Actually, I have a few things we need to go over. Perhaps we can do it then."

"Oh, goody!" Madeleine said excitedly. "I like things!"

The elevator opened on the first floor and Cameron stepped out, holding the door with one arm for Madeleine. But she remained, rifling through her purse. "You coming?" Cameron inquired.

Madeleine smiled and shook her head. "No—you go on without me." Her hand dove back into her purse and extracted a compact. She reached out and pushed the button that read "MOM" and the doors began to close.

"Oh, wait!" Cameron said, jamming his arm back into the door, causing it to reopen. He dug in his front pocket and pulled out the receipt for Madeleine's merchandise. "This is for your bedding and stuff."

Madeleine reached out and took the receipt from the expectant Cameron and dropped it in her purse without reading it. "Thank you!" she said appreciatively. She gave him a little finger wave as the elevator doors drew shut.

CHAPTER THIRTEEN

CAMERON SAT ON THE soft leather couch in his living room with his feet on the coffee table, a rerun on the television in front of him. Chewbacca looked asleep on the floor, but one open eye was dutifully tracking the invisible intruder on the wall.

Cameron thought about his morning with Madeleine and the store which could seemingly do nothing right. *How do they stay in business?* Cameron didn't really know anything about retailing, but so much of what they were doing wrong seemed so, well, *obvious*. He recalled the two customers behind him discussing how much they disliked shopping in the store. He had heard two similar conversations in the short time he was there. *How can you not know your customers hate you so much?*

"I suppose it's not really that much different than Household Solutions, is it?" he asked Chewbacca. "I guess it's only been a week since we learned how much our customers dislike us." He winced as a thought struck him. "Are we really that bad?" Visions of a woman scaling the Household Solutions building, trying to buy an electric can opener, flashed in front of him. "We can't be *that* bad, can we?"

Chewbacca opened both eyes wide and turned his head to Cameron. The dog misinterpreted his owner's pained expression and jumped up excitedly. With a single, deep *wroof*, he sprinted to the door. Cameron winced again as he heard the sound of skidding, followed by the muffled thud of dog hitting door.

"Coming!" Cameron said, heaving himself off the couch. "Go get your leash," he ordered. There was the scrambling of paws on hardwood as Chewbacca made his way to the laundry room where it was kept. He smiled as his companion reappeared with the brown, drool-covered, leather leash in his mouth. "Yuck," he said as he hooked it on the collar.

Chewbacca tilted his head and looked at Cameron questioningly. *Wrong leash?*

As they walked, Cameron thought about the ideas the senior management team had presented. Adding value, improving processes, improving skills of the employees, improving accessibility. They all made sense now, but something was missing. What was it Madeleine had said on that first day about the books he had bought? "You're getting every perspective except one—the most important one." He shook his head. Intuitively, he knew she was right. He was missing something. But what?

The other end of the leash tugged suddenly, causing Cameron to lurch forward. Chewbacca had spied a squirrel hanging on the side of a tree and thought it would make a fun playmate. Cameron regained his balance and held tight to the leash. Chewbacca looked disappointedly back at Cameron. He tried one more time, just in case Cameron wasn't serious, but apparently he was. The squirrel watched with amusement as his would-be assailant was restrained. Chewbacca trotted off to his left, pretending to ignore him.

CHAPTER FOURTEEN

ON HIS WAY TO the Saggezza Center the next morning, Cameron stopped at the office. He was getting used to this early morning routine. The good coffee was on, although there was no sign of Gerard.

The first thing he noticed when he walked into his office was the note placed in the middle of his desk.

Cam: Got some ideas about that experience thing you're working on. See me. Stan. So Stan had some ideas. Cameron pursed his lips. Normally, he would have welcomed this, but lately Stan hadn't been tremendously supportive. Cameron wondered if these ideas were actually going to be helpful.

He found two more messages in his inbox after firing up his computer. The first was from Susan Tremmel in HR, advising him that she was going to move forward with the university idea. The second was from CFO Gayle Humphries letting him know they planned to implement the tiered customer structure. Cameron frowned. This was getting awkward.

He hit reply, then typed in, *Thanks for the update Gayle. Can we sit on this for a week or so until I have a better handle on things?*

He sent a similar reply to Tremmel. He sat back and sighed.

Nothing like starting your day by throwing cold water on peoples' initiatives.

It was just before 8:30 when Cameron left the office to meet Madeleine. When he got to the Santee Alley area, he headed to the parking garage he'd found the day before, and by chance ended up in the very same space. He smiled to himself as he realized how happy even this little bit of routineness made him.

He made it to the Saggezza Centre ten minutes early, and already there was a small line by the door. He stood outside to wait for Madeleine and looked up at the building. It was odd for a shopping center. It didn't look like one. Aside from the small name plate above the door, it gave no indication as to what it was. No window displays, no signs. Yet, as he observed from the crowd beginning to grow, a lot of people seemed to know it.

Cameron had decided he would push Madeleine for something a little more concrete today. While the excursion to the mall had been interesting, he wasn't really sure it related to the manufacturing business, or how it was going to help him develop a strategic plan. *I better come up with something soon,* he thought, *or I'm going to look like an idiot. Especially now that I've told a SVP and CFO to stop their initiatives.*

He had spent much of the prior evening reviewing Household Solutions' overall presence. Aside from fairly small things, such as the website issue Stan had raised, Cameron couldn't really find anything that looked horribly wrong to him. Obviously, he was missing something, but he couldn't for the life of him figure out what it was. The biggest problem was not knowing where to look.

Just then, he caught a glimpse of a fitted hat in white lace bobbing down the street toward him. As it got closer, he could see Madeleine had yet again changed her look, this time to full 1920s flapper. White sequined top, black three-layered skirt with frills at the bottom. She had accessorized her ensemble with two long pearl necklaces and matching earrings. Her now jet-black hair stood in blazing contrast to it all.

She smiled when she saw Cameron. Still a full twenty feet away, when she started talking to him, hands flipping in emphasis, her frilly, white, sequined purse swaying under her arm. she let loose with a streaming monologue: "So I was thinking all night about that iced raspberry cappuccino—it was driving me CRAZY. So you'd think I'd want one when I woke up, right? Wrong! When I woke up, I suddenly NEEDED a mint caramel latte and banana-cranberry biscotti! It's not even an option anymore. If I don't get one soon, I'm going to fall over and die. It's just that important. But then I thought, 'Oh no, I have to meet you here this morning,' which really depressed me—not because I didn't want to meet you—but because I really, really need a mint caramel latte and banana-cranberry biscotti. Then I remembered that Gino just opened up a new café just up the street, which made me VERY happy! So we're off to CappuGino's before we do anything. I hope you don't mind. You can try their new Chili-ccino—it's amazing!"

Cameron couldn't help but smile as she neared, prattling and gesturing away, seemingly oblivious of the crowd around them. He expected Madeleine to at least stop to shake his hand, but she didn't even break stride. He felt the breeze on his face as she marched past him and down the sidewalk. He hurried to catch up. When he did, Madeleine interrupted her happy chatter. "So, have you figured out what Household Solutions' problem is yet?"

Cameron blinked. "What do you mean?" he asked

"Well, you've had some time to think about it," she said matter-of-factly. "Have you figured out what the problem is yet?"

"No, I haven't," said Cameron honestly. "But isn't that what I hired you for? To tell me what we're doing wrong and how to fix it?"

"Exactly my point," Madeleine said in agreement. "So tell me what Household Solutions is doing wrong."

"Madeleine, I said I don't know!" Cameron said, exasperated. "You tell me!"

Cameron was already three strides ahead when he realized Madeleine had stopped. The look on her face reminded him of his third grade teacher when she was having to repeat something for the fourth time. "It's *Maddy*," she said. "Which, I should point out, I've already explained."

Once again, Cameron found himself trying to regain his equilibrium. "Yeah . . . but . . ." he began.

"*Yabut* is the cry of the closed-minded," Madeleine interrupted with admonishment. "When you open your eyes, ears, and your mind, it's amazing how many answers are right there in front of you." Before Cameron could reply, she looked up at the building beside them, placed both hands on her hips, and smiled widely. "Oh, *very* nice Gino!" she said, nodding in approval. Cameron hadn't even noticed they had reached their destination. The café had faux terracotta walls, with a green and white striped awning overhead. Above the awning was the sign reading *CappuGino's*. The U was shaped into a stylized coffee cup. Above the sign were three brightly-colored, shuttered windows with overflowing flower boxes.

On the sidewalk were three marble-topped tables surrounded by white wicker chairs. A couple was just standing to leave, and Madeleine moved forward to claim the empty table. "This is his newest café," she said to Cameron. "Gino tells me the rents here are more than double anywhere else, but that it's worth it because of the traffic."

A young waitress appeared beside them as they took their seats. "Good morning!" she said cheerfully. "What can I get for you today?" As she spoke, she looked at Madeleine, and recognition slowly dawned. "Oh, goodness, are you *Maddy*?" she asked with excitement. Madeleine looked up at her with her twinkling green eyes. *Wait,* Cameron thought. *Green?* But . . .

"I am," Madeleine said to the young server. "I'm terribly sorry, have we met?"

"Oh, no, not at all," the girl said enthusiastically, "but Gino insists that we have to know all of our best customers. There's a picture of you and Gino posted in the back room, with a note that you are our absolute, most important customer." She paused to think for a moment. "Wait! Let me guess," she said holding a finger up. "You'd like a double espresso infused with maple mango, and a black forest ham tea biscuit!" she said triumphantly. "Am I right?"

Madeleine actually blushed. "Oh, my goodness," she said to the girl, "I feel like a positive CELEBRITY! And I do LOVE the maple mango espresso!" The waitress beamed. Madeleine leaned forward conspiratorially. "But today, I am absolutely DESPERATE for a mint caramel latte and banana-cranberry biscotti. Can you do that for me?"

"Of course!" the girl replied brightly, and made a note on her pad. She turned her smile to Cameron, and asked, "and for you sir?"

Cameron thought for a moment, then said, "I'll have the Chili-ccino," he said, recalling Madeleine's recommendation. The waitress dutifully wrote down the order, then disappeared inside the front door. Moments later she appeared with a worried look on her face.

"I am so sorry!" she said apologetically. "It looks like it might take an extra five minutes to get your order. Is that okay? You said you were desperate for the latte, so I feel just awful!"

Madeleine gave her a comforting smile and patted her hand. "I think we can manage the wait." She paused to look at the waitresses name badge. "Angie."

Angie gave her a thankful smile, then excused herself to attend to another table.

"Wow," Cameron said, impressed, "Gino certainly thinks very highly of you. What did you do for him?"

"Oh, not very much, really," Madeleine said modestly. "He gives me far too much credit for his success. He's very bright, you know." She paused for a moment, once again locking him into her gaze. "And so are you, young man," she said with one eyebrow raised pointedly. "You have a lot of potential. You just have to start looking at things the right way, that's all. So let's start again. Tell me what you know about the customer experience problems at Household Solutions."

Cameron sat back in his chair. "That's what I'm trying to figure out," he said, the frustration back in his voice. "The senior people in our office seem to think we need to improve our training, our processes, our communications, our added value. They all make sense, but I don't have a clue where to start."

"Well, certainly not in those places," Madeleine said with a wave of her hand. "Oh, I have no doubt those are things you might have to look at when it's time to *fix* the problem. But that's not the question I've been asking. What is the problem?"

Cameron thought for a moment. "I've been struggling with that. Aside from a few things that need to be fixed with our website, improving our delivery percentage—those types of things—I'm not sure."

"Again," said Madeleine, "you're talking about what needs to be fixed, but not telling me what the problem is." Cameron shook his head, still not understanding. Madeleine put her purse on the table and leaned closer to him. "Let's look at it this way. You know why you are embarking on this whole customer experience mission, right?" she asked. Cameron nodded.

"Well?" she asked expectantly.

"Because if we don't, Household Solutions is in trouble," Cameron said.

There was an audible thud as Madeleine's head hit the table theatrically. She tilted her head to look up at him over the top of her black and white Louis Vuitton glasses. Cameron looked back, unsure what to say. "What?" he finally said

"Why," Madeleine spoke slowly and deliberately, "do you think you need to improve your customer experience?"

"Because our customers don't like us," answered Cameron.

"Ah! And why," Madeleine continued, feigning patience, "don't your customers like you?"

"Because their experience is horrible?" said Cameron. Thud, thud, thud from the other side of the table.

Angie's cheerful expression was a little unsure as she approached the puzzled, well-dressed businessman, and the older, eccentric-looking woman who was banging her head repeatedly on the table. She cleared her throat as she approached. Madeleine paused and looked up at the tray.

Her face brightened, and she sat up with excitement. "Perfect timing!" she exclaimed, whisking her latte from the tray before Angie had a chance to serve it to her. She held it in both hands, and inhaled the steam deeply. "Ah!" she said, "perfect!" She looked back at the tray as Angie handed Cameron his cup, and her face fell. "But the biscotti! Where is the biscotti?"

"It should be here any minute," said Angie apologetically. "I wanted to serve both together, but the latte and Chili-ccino were ready, and I didn't want them to get cold while we waited."

"Waiting for a biscotti?" Madeleine asked. "Don't you just have to take one out of the case? Aren't they pre-made?"

"Well, normally, yes," came the reply, "but, you see . . ."

Just then, a young blond man wearing a CappuGino's uniform materialized out of the crowd of shoppers that were now filling the street. He had a careful and gentle grip on a small white cardboard box as he hurried toward the restaurant. Angie waved to him, and he wove his way to the table.

"Thank you *so* much, Paul!" Angie said with relief when he arrived. "I owe you one!"

"Anything for you Ang!" the young man said with a smile. With a small wave to Cameron and Madeleine, he turned and jogged away. Angie opened the box, and with a pair of tongs, carefully lifted out two biscottis and placed them on the plates. Turning to Madeleine, she explained, "we were all out of banana-cranberry biscotti, so I called Paul. He works in the CappuGino's on South Main—it's about six blocks away. They had some that were just fresh made, so he ran it over."

Cameron looked at the biscotti, and at Angie in amazement. "Wow," he said to Madeleine, "you must *really* be important!"

"She *is*!" Angie said to Cameron. "But we do this all the time. All of our customers are important to us." She turned to Madeleine and continued, "I'm just happy that I was able to find them for you. I know how much you were looking forward to them."

Madeleine smiled at Angie and took a dainty bite out of the banana-cranberry biscotti. Her face melted in ecstasy. "Oooo," she moaned. "You have MADE my morning! Thank you, dear!"

Angie beamed. The happy waitress excused herself and Cameron sat back in his chair, thinking about what he had just experienced. Maddy was savoring her long-awaited latte and biscotti. "Now *this* is an outstanding experience," Cameron said aloud. "Even I can see that. But how do I translate this into my business?"

Madeleine dabbed the biscotti crumbs off her lips and looked at Cameron with a smile. "Nom dear, no. What you experienced here was quite different than outstanding experience."

"What do you mean?" Cameron asked, furrowing his eyebrows. "If this isn't an outstanding customer experience, then what is?"

Madeleine laughed loud enough for the other patrons to look their way. "Oh, don't get me wrong. CappuGinos' customer experience is indeed outstanding. I just wouldn't call *this* an example of outstanding experience. But you're not nearly ready for *that* lesson yet!" she said. "With any luck, you might be there some day, but not today!"

Cameron squinted in confusion. Madeleine crunched down on another piece, and Cameron could see that her eyes had regained the twinkle. "Baby steps, Cameron. Baby steps. For goodness sake, you haven't even learned why your customers don't like you yet! I'm thinking that's probably step one, don't you?"

She finished off the last of her biscotti and leaned forward again. "We really must get back to the store!" she said. "They have energy efficient bulbs on sale for half price, and I don't want to miss out. But before we do, I want to go back to that question you keep avoiding. Why don't your customers like doing business with you?"

"Hey!" Cameron cried, "I am not avoiding that question. I keep trying to answer it, and all you do is bang your head on the table!"

"Oh, *great* answers," Madeleine said with no attempt to conceal the sarcasm. "You think you need to improve your customer experience because your customers don't like you. And when I ask why they don't like you, you answer that it's because you need to improve your customer experience! My head is spinning just thinking about it—you're talking in circles!"

She was right, Cameron knew. He nodded and shrugged. "Okay, so what's the answer?" he asked. "Because I have no idea."

"My point EXACTLY!" Madeleine exclaimed. She stood and smiled. "NOW we're making progress! So let's go shopping!" She deftly reached into the breast pocket of Cameron's jacket and plucked out his wallet. Fishing out a twenty dollar bill and setting it under one of the plates, she said cheerfully, "I think she deserves a good tip, don't you?"

"Um, sure," Cameron muttered dazedly as Madeleine handed the wallet back. He closed his eyes tightly, then opened them and looked around. *Nope. Not a dream.*

"What do you mean, *exactly*?" he finally blurted out as he chased after her. "All I said is that I have no idea!"

"Right!" said Madeleine, dodging around a vendor holding out an imitation Prada purse for inspection. "So now you've narrowed the scope of places to look for answers by eliminating yourself as a possible source. So the question you have to ask yourself is, who does know?"

Cameron managed to keep pace with her on the right side. "You?" he guessed.

Madeleine stopped abruptly, and watched Cameron walk face first into a trolley of hanging garments. Cameron, garments, and trolley all tumbled onto the street. She absentmindedly adjusted her hat and smoothed her skirt as Cameron extracted himself from the pile and made his apologies to the agitated clothier.

"You?" Cameron asked Madeleine again, once he had regained his footing.

"Don't be silly!" Madeleine replied. "What do I know about Household Solutions?" She resumed walking and looked straight forward.

"Okay, I give up!" Cameron said with exasperation. "Who?"

They had reached the Saggezza Center. Madeleine opened the door and stepped into the foyer. "No more questions!" she pronounced. "It's time for shopping!"

"No, wait!" Cameron exclaimed, stopping in his tracks. "Madeleine . . . er . . . Maddy," he quickly corrected himself as she gave him a stern look, "I don't want to go shopping! I've got to fix our customer experience. I don't have time to traipse around stores all day."

Madeleine looked at him over her glasses. "Pity," she said, and then added cryptically, "because you really can't have one without the other, you know." She started walking toward the door to the elevators, then stopped at the door and turned. "Come," she said, "join me for one more day." She waited expectantly.

Cameron stood, thinking for a moment. He remembered Gerard's words. *My friend says she's the best. Learn as much from her as you can.* He sighed and began walking toward her. *Might as well. It's not like I really have a Plan B at this stage,* he thought.

Just before he got to the door, he said to Madeleine, "Why are we using the elevator? Why don't we just go on this floor?" He indicated the glass doors leading into the store in front of them.

"Oh, pish," came the reply. "You're not ready for that floor yet. Baby steps . . ."

CHAPTER FIFTEEN

THE ELEVATOR DOORS OPENED, and the same scene as the day before appeared in front of them. Merchandise was scattered, boxes were opened, aisles were clogged, and customers were navigating the landscape like skiers on a slalom course. "You take a look around. A *good* look," said Madeleine. "I'm heading for the light bulbs. Meet you at the cash in an hour?"

"It's going to take you an hour to find the light bulbs?" Cameron asked.

Madeleine grinned and said, "No, but it may take you that long to see the things you need to see. I'm sure I can find *something* to keep myself occupied." Cameron nodded. He was sure she could.

As Madeleine disappeared into the maze of shelves and merchandise, Cameron began wandering around again. The first aisle he traversed was lined with shelves filled with packages of diapers. Two women were standing in the center having an animated discussion. They both appeared to be in their twenties and obviously knew each other. One had short, dark, curly hair and was dressed in jeans and a collared t-shirt. The other had slightly lighter hair, pulled into a loose, shoulder-length pony tail. She was wearing shorts and a sleeveless top. Each held two bundles of diapers in their hands.

"Oh, you're absolutely right," the woman with the ponytail was saying. "They're at least three dollars cheaper than anywhere else I've seen them. I'm just not sure I want to wait the twenty minutes in line. It might not be so bad if they had carts—at least that way you're not having to hold them. And if they had carts, I'd probably be buying even more. I will never understand why they don't have them here."

"No kidding," the curly-haired woman replied. "And if they had carts, we could use them to stand on to get the things we want from those incredibly high shelves." They both laughed and looked up at the shelves beside them.

"I know!" ponytail said. "The last time I was here, I carried a broom around with me to knock the things off the top shelf I needed. I remember swearing then I would never come back to this store. I'm not even sure why I'm here now."

"You and me both," curly hair said. "Hey, let's get out of here and grab a coffee. I hear CappuGino's has a new, low-fat, iced toffee-ccino that will just take your breath away! So you spend an extra three bucks on diapers someplace else. Who cares?"

"I'm in!" ponytail agreed enthusiastically. She stuffed her bundles back on the shelves, and the two of them walked away.

Cameron stood and watched them go. *How does this place stay in business?* he thought to himself one more time. As he turned to head down the next aisle, he was confronted by a middle-aged man with dark hair, a goatee, and thick, gold glasses. Cameron placed him at fortyish—around the same age as himself. The man had a confused look and was holding a Household Solutions Fruit-Washer box in his hand.

"Can you help me?" the man asked Cameron. "My wife asked me to pick this up. I wandered around for half an hour until I found one. I stood in line for the cash for another fifteen minutes—because apparently the self-serve counters aren't working today—and when I finally get there, it doesn't scan into their scanner. The woman at the cash, who looks like she hasn't smiled since she was three years old, tells me that the only way I'll be able to buy it is if I come back and tell her what the actual price and code are. The problem is, I'm not sure where to look for them. I found my way back to the place I spotted this one, but there are no others around. It's like someone just dropped it there. Do you have any idea where I might look or how much these things are?"

Cameron looked at the box in the man's hand. "That's last year's model, so I'm not sure what they might be selling it for," he said apologetically. "And I'm afraid I can't help you in finding out where the prices might be. I really don't know my way around here very well."

The man visibly sagged at the prospect of continuing his search. An idea struck Cameron. "I do know that they carry them at Hilda's Home Stores, though," he said to the man. "There's one around my house, and I've seen the Fruit-Washer there for $44.95. They'll have the newer model too—and it's quite improved over last year's."

At this, the man brightened. "Thanks!" he said. "There's a Hilda's Home not too far from me. I just work near here and thought I'd check this place out. Bad idea, I guess." He smiled appreciatively at Cameron and set the box on a nearby empty shelf. "I'm guessing since you know so much about this thing that you must own one?" he asked.

"Well, I actually work at Household Solutions. We're the ones who manufacture the Fruit-Washer," Cameron said with a smile. "My team designed this," he added with a touch of pride in his voice.

The man looked at Cameron with an appraising eye. "You work at Household Solutions, huh?" he said finally. "Then I'm even more surprised I was able to get any help from you." And with that, he turned and walked away, Cameron staring after him.

CHAPTER SIXTEEN

CAMERON STOOD IN THE aisle, thinking about the man's parting comment. *Are we really that bad?* Why hadn't he seen this before? He began to walk up and down the unmarked aisles, scanning the merchandise. A few minutes later, he found himself in what probably passed for the kitchenware section.

He looked at the merchandise haphazardly stacked on the shelves. Sure enough, there were a number of Household Solutions products there, surrounded by similar products from the competitors. *Actually,* Cameron thought, *a lot of products from the competitors.* Why weren't there more Household Solutions products there? Emily Seabourne's words hit him like a wave of ice water. The consultant was right. Only the new Household Solutions products seemed to be in stock. *How long,* Cameron thought, *before they too were overshadowed by the competition?*

A couple came down the aisle and Cameron stepped aside as they began peering at the coffee makers. They looked to both be in their mid-twenties, and from their accents, Cameron guessed that they were natives of New England.

"Oh, look," the man said. "They've got that new Household Solutions Ice Cream Cake Maker! This would be perfect for the kids' birthday parties."

The woman leaned closer to take a look. "I've heard about this. It's supposed to be really good," she said. "It's really too bad you can't make the cakes into different shapes other than round, though."

"But you can," the man exclaimed, pointing at the pictures on the side of the box. "It says here you can buy six different three-dimensional molds—star, dome, whale, baseball diamond and castle." He looked around to see if any were visible on the nearby shelves. Nothing. "I don't see any of them here, but I'm sure you can order them from the company."

The woman laughed, took the box from her companion and placed it back on the shelf. She patted the back of his hand. "That's a Household Solutions product, honey. Don't count on it."

Cameron flushed as they walked away. This was embarrassing. Moments later, it got worse.

A woman with long auburn hair came around the corner and headed straight for the coffee makers. At the same time, two other people came into the area. One began looking at microwaves, the other at the bar fridges. Cameron was pleased to see that each had gone first to the respective Household Solutions product.

Just then, a stern-looking woman in her mid-fifties walked by. She stopped and spoke loud enough for everyone else to take notice. "WhatEVER you do, don't buy anything made by THAT company! Not unless you LIKE migraines, that is . . ."

The other woman, startled, looked down at the Household Solutions Heat-Surround Slow Cooker in her hand. "What's wrong with it?" she asked curiously.

"It's made by Household Solutions, that's what's wrong with it! Oh, sure, it might work great. But if it breaks, you might as well just burn it. Don't even think about them honoring the warranty. The store will tell you to send it back to the manufacturer, and *these* clowns will give you such a runaround that your head will spin. That's their game. They figure that eventually you'll give up and go away. You're better off just not buying anything from them in the first place!"

At this, all three people set their respective products down. "Thanks," said the man who had been eyeing the SlimFridge. "That helps me with my decision." He picked up one of the competitor's products, heaved it onto his shoulder, and walked away.

Cameron began to say something, then thought better of it. The woman, satisfied she'd been heard, disappeared into the next aisle. The two other would-be customers left empty-handed.

Cameron stood there for a long time, thinking about what he had just witnessed. He was catching a glimpse of Household Solutions he had never seen before, and he didn't like it. Lost in thought, he made his way toward the front of the store.

As he neared the front, he could see the same cashier, listlessly processing merchandise. The line was only about twelve people deep, and he scanned it for Madeleine. He spied her at the very front of the line, standing beside an impossibly tall stack of light bulbs and other miscellanea. She was intently reading one of the gossip magazines from a nearby rack. Cameron made his way up to her, eyeing the bulbs with one eyebrow raised. "You must have a very bright house."

Madeleine looked up from her magazine and perked up. "I try to shed as much light on things as I can," she said, matching his straight face. Then she smiled. "Here, you guard my stash, and I'll get us a cart."

Three minutes later, Cameron was disassembling the stack and placing the items on the conveyor belt. He looked up for Madeleine, but there was no sign of her. When he was done, he pulled his wallet out and waited to hear the damage. Still no Madeleine. *The woman's got great timing, if nothing else,* he thought.

He viewed the items as the cashier inexorably plodded through them. Twenty-three boxes of LED bulbs, a pewter and glass beer mug, three brightly-colored pashminas, a digital picture frame, a crystal piggy bank, and a 30-piece set of china plates. When finished, the cashier's flat voice announced the price, and Cameron again gave her his credit card. He'd have to deduct this, he thought, from Madeleine's bill.

As if on cue, Madeleine appeared with the cart. They loaded it, and Cameron began walking to the elevator. Madeleine, as it turned out, had other ideas. "What's your hurry?" she asked, not moving.

Cameron shrugged. "None, I guess." He was actually quite anxious to talk with her about his experiences that morning, and thought they might do it over another Chili-ccino, which he had quite enjoyed.

"There's someone I think you need to talk to," Madeleine explained. "Follow me." She strode purposefully to the left side of the storefront, to the door from which the security guards had appeared the day before. Cameron trailed behind obediently.

CHAPTER SEVENTEEN

MADELEINE HELD THE DOOR for Cameron as he pushed the cart into one of the dingiest waiting rooms he had ever seen. The walls were gray, the carpet was a faded brown, and the furniture looked like it had been picked up in a rummage sale fifty years ago.

At the dull wooden reception desk sat a woman who might have been the twin of the cashier out front. She matched the walls. Everything about her was gray. Her suit, her hair, her eyes—even her skin seemed gray. When Madeleine approached her, she raised her head slightly and looked at her with a bored expression.

"Good morning!" Madeleine said cheerfully. "I was wondering if I might have a few moments of Mr. Langsam's time. Tell him it's Maddy and a friend."

Without acknowledging that Madeleine had spoken, the receptionist punched a button on her console. "Maddy is here to see you," she said after a moment. A few seconds later, she punched another button to disconnect the call and looked back up. "He's busy," she said brusquely. "If you want to wait, he'll be about fifteen minutes."

"That would be fine," Madeleine responded with a smile, seemingly oblivious to the receptionist's cool demeanor. She took Cameron's hand and led him to the shabby couch. The entire place had a heavy air to it. In the background, Cameron could hear the faint sound of a telephone ring three times, stop for a few moments, then ring three more times, then stop.

"So," she said as they seated themselves. "What have we learned so far today?"

Cameron looked down at his shoes for a moment, then up at Madeleine. "Quite a lot, I think," he said quietly, "but I haven't had time to figure out what it means yet." He described to her the events of the morning. Madeleine listened intently

"It's frustrating," he said. "I feel as though I'm getting to see a bunch of random pieces of a puzzle, but none of them fit together yet. I don't even know what the ultimate picture looks like. I know what I'm seeing is important, but I'm not sure what to do about them or how they fit into the big picture." He looked at Madeleine, who returned his gaze with an appreciative smile.

"That's a good feeling to have," she said.

Cameron raised an eyebrow. "No, really!" she insisted. "Most people already assume they know what the picture looks like, and then try to jam the puzzle pieces into places they think they should be—whether they fit or not. Then they hold their completed puzzle up for the world to see, jagged and imperfect, believing they've found a truth. It may be frustrating for you now, but when things do start to come together, you will at least be seeing what's really there, instead of seeing the things you *want* to see."

Cameron nodded. It was small consolation to his frustration, but it was something. He thought in silence for a few moments. "Maddy," he asked finally, "when we first met and I told you about the books I'd bought, you said I was getting every perspective except one—the most important one. What is the perspective I'm missing? That's the key, isn't it?"

"Oh, VERY good question!" Madeleine said, eyes twinkling. "There's hope for you yet!" She checked her watch and began to stand.

"No, wait," Cameron said, grabbing her arm. "I don't have time to play games. Telling me I'm asking good questions isn't helping me."

Madeleine sat back down and turned to him. "But your

questions are important." She was serious, and for the first time, Cameron could see the depth behind the brightness of her eyes.

"But I don't need questions. I need answers," he said. "Look, I have to come up with a plan soon. This has all been very educational, and I have no doubt it will help. Right now, Maddy, I really need answers."

Madeleine regarded him thoughtfully for a few moments. "Cameron," she said, tilting her head to one side, "what size of electric motor goes in an appliance?"

Cameron blinked. "What?" he asked. "What does that have to do with . . .

"It has *everything* to do with our discussion," Madeleine interrupted seriously. "Now tell me—what size of electric motor goes in an appliance?"

"Well, it depends," Cameron said, starting to get a little annoyed, "on the kind of appliance. I mean, what's the size? What will the motor be running? How long will it run for? What are the loads? There are a lot of factors."

"Cameron," Madeleine said slowly. "I didn't ask you for questions. I asked you for an answer." She kept her gaze on him, expectantly.

"But . . ." Cameron's mouth snapped shut as Madeleine's point hit home. He flushed.

"Cameron, there's no point in trying to come up with answers until you're sure you're asking the right questions," Madeleine said. "I understand your urgency, but the truth is, getting the questions right is ninety percent of the battle." She turned so that her whole body was facing him. The frills on her lace hat danced. "Customer experience and customer service are all too often taken for granted. People think that just because they recognize a good customer experience when they see it, they understand how to deliver it in their own organization.

"It's like someone thinking they can bake a great cake just because they recognize one when they see it. Or someone thinking they can build a house just because they can swing a hammer. It doesn't work like that. Nor can you just find some kind of paint-by-number users guide to customer experience and apply it to any organization.

"What's the term you corporate folks like to use? Oh yes—best practices—that's what you call them. More like risky practices usually. I mean, they might have been a best practice for one organization, but they could be useless to another. A templated approach can only take you so far. People think of customer experience as being something simplistic, easy, uncomplicated. But if it was really all that straight-forward, why are so few organizations really good at it? Some people will tell you that it's just common sense, but that's nonsense," Madeleine continued in earnest, her eyes boring into his. "What seems to be common sense for one person might be seen by somebody with a different vantage point as the silliest thing in the world.

"Customer experience isn't a *thing*, Cameron," she continued. "It's a perception. And it changes depending on the customer and the organization. If you want to deliver it, you first have to identify what it looks like." She paused and patted his arm. "Once you've identified it, the answers you're looking for are much easier to see."

Cameron looked up at Madeleine, and saw the earnestness in her eyes. There was a depth to this woman that transcended the eccentric clothes and quirkiness. He saw that now, too. And she was right. Despite the pressure from his CEO, there was no point in trying to come up with answers until he knew the right questions to ask. "So, what now?" he asked finally.

Madeleine gave him a warm smile, and her eyes resumed their twinkle. "Well," she said, "for starters, I think we've waited here long enough."

She stood and smoothed the layers of her skirt. "Let's go in, shall we?" She pushed her shopping cart up by the reception desk and said to the stone-faced receptionist, "Be a dear, would you, and watch this for us?" Not waiting for an answer, she turned and walked to the door leading to the inner offices, opened it, and held it for Cameron. "After you," she said with a flourish of an arm. Cameron glanced back to the receptionist, who appeared oblivious of Madeleine's boldness, then walked through the door, bowing slightly to Madeleine as he passed.

They stood in a long gray hallway that had a number of other gray hallways branching off from it to the right and left. There were no signs, no landmarks. Nothing that might indicate what was where.

Like a rat in a maze, Cameron thought. He heard the ringing telephone again, this time a little louder. Three rings, stop, three rings, stop. He realized it had probably been ringing constantly since they had first entered the office. He had just tuned it out. *That's got to make for an annoying work environment.*

Wordlessly, they began walking further into the bowels of the maze. The ever-present sound of the ringing telephone began to get much louder, as they were obviously approaching its source. Madeleine turned right down an aisle, then made another right. *How are we ever going to find our way back?* Cameron thought. He suddenly stopped and stared in an office to his left. Madeleine halted and came back to see what had piqued his interest.

The office was a nondescript ten-by-ten room with a file cabinet against the wall beside a plain wooden desk and chair. On a square table in the middle of the room was a single telephone, hooked up to an old computer. The telephone rang three times, then stopped. Cameron could hear the click as the call was routed to the CPU. From the computer's internal speaker, he could make out the message. "Thank you for calling," a bored female voice spoke. "Unfortunately all of our agents are busy at the moment. Your call is important to us, so please hold, and we will be with you shortly."

Cameron could hear a music track begin, then the sound switched off and the telephone rang again. Three rings. "Thank you for calling . . ." Cameron couldn't help himself. Drawn to the scene like a moth to a flame, he walked over to the computer monitor. On the screen was a dashboard showing the call history and current call statistics.

The first showed the current date—April 5, and the calls month-to-date—1,353. That worked out to over two hundred calls a day. It seemed to be a lot for a retail operation. He actually did a double-take at the next number, though. *Calls answered: zero.* He scanned the other statistics. *Current calls in queue: thirty-six. Average wait time: twenty-two minutes. Calls escalated: Zero.*

Cameron spied a headset hooked to the side of the CPU and, on a whim, put it on. He punched a button on the keyboard to listen to one of the calls. Nothing but the telephone music track. He pushed another button. More music. *Are none of these calls really being answered?* He pushed a third button, and found himself in the middle of a verbal barrage forcing him to hold the headset away from his ear. "ANSWER YOUR @#$% TELEPHONE!" a man's voice penetrated the earpiece and into the room. "THIS IS THE TENTH TIME I'VE CALLED, AND THERE IS NO @#$% WAY I'M SITTING ON HOLD FOR ANOTHER HALF HOUR! I CAN'T BELIEVE THIS! YOU PEOPLE ARE SO @#$% USELESS . . ."

Cameron cringed and punched another number. Over the music, he could hear a woman's voice, ". . . yeah, I'm still on hold . . . twenty minutes already . . . I know, but the cashier said the only way I could return it is by talking to customer service, and this is the number she gave me . . . Yes, I know . . . I *have* tried other numbers, but they all come back to this line . . . Yeah, you're right . . . I'm just going to give it another five minutes, then try again tomorrow . . ."

Cameron took the headset off and looked up at Madeleine. She was standing by the door with a compact in one hand, adjusting her makeup. "What is this place?" Cameron asked her. *Ring, ring, ring,* the phone chirped beside him. *Thank you for calling . . .*

Madeleine dug her lipstick out of her purse and looked at Cameron. "I believe this is their customer support center," she said matter-of-factly. "That would be my guess, anyway." She dabbed at her lips.

"But it looks like they never actually answer their phone," Cameron said, gesturing to the monitor. "What kind of support center is this?"

Madeleine smacked her lips together and peered in her small mirror to make sure everything was the way it should be. She turned to Cameron with a raised eyebrow. "What kind of support center would you be expecting?" she asked.

"But . . ." Cameron began, then thought the better of it. *Ring, ring, ring. Thank you for calling . . .*

Madeleine clicked her purse shut and looked at him. "Are you quite finished?" she asked. "We do have an appointment, you know."

Cameron nodded dumbly and walked to the doorway, eyes still transfixed on the telephone. *Unbelievable.*

CHAPTER EIGHTEEN

TWO MORE CORRIDORS LATER, they were standing in front of a large gray door, with a brass sign reading, *S. R. Langsam, General Manager.* Madeleine knocked softly on the door. There was no response from inside, and she knocked again. Still nothing. They waited for another twenty seconds. Madeleine gave Cameron a knowing smile, then reached for the doorknob and pushed the door open.

The office was huge but sparse. Seated behind an enormous desk was a straight-backed, stick-like man. The pin-striped suit accentuated his thin arms and neck and created an even greater contrast to a very large, very round head. He had fine, angular, pinched features and impossibly round eyes framed with equally round, thick, gold glasses. The effect created an illusion of eyeballs sitting on top of his face, instead of recessed in eye sockets. The prominent dark hair semi-circling the large bald spot on the top of his head finished off the look to create an almost comic strip image.

He looked at them with annoyance. "May I help you?" he said thinly. He didn't really sound as though he wanted to help.

Madeleine stepped forward. "S.R.?" she said. "Don't you recognize me? It's Maddy!" Cameron was surprised to see that not only did the stickman not brighten at the sight of Madeleine, he actually appeared to become even more annoyed. This was a first.

"Oh, I recognize you," he said flatly. "And I don't remember asking you to be sent in."

"Oh, pish," said Madeleine with a wave of her hand. "You're a busy man. You can't be expected to remember everything." She walked forward to the desk and said, "This is Cameron Whitehall, from Household Solutions." Cameron walked forward and extended his hand. The stick man peered at him through his glasses, his eyes appearing to dance on the surface of his head. He half-stood and half-heartedly shook Cameron's hand.

"S.R. Langsam," he said, seating himself again right away. His faint accent—Cameron guessed German—made it sound like 'Sehr Langsam.'

Madeleine sat down in one of the visitor chairs in front of Langsam. Cameron followed suit. Langsam glared at Madeleine. "So, what is it now?" he said contemptuously. "Another return? Another pricing error? Another complaint about us not having what you saw in the flyer? Oh, wait, let me guess. You've brought Mr. Whitehall here because you bought a defective Household Solutions product and they're tired of dealing with you, too." He turned to Cameron. "Is that it? You're just here to make sure I don't send our favorite customer back to you for a warranty claim?"

The word 'favorite' dripped with sarcasm.

Cameron just looked at Langsam, not quite sure what to say. Madeleine cut in. "Actually," she said with a sweet smile, "I just thought you might be willing to let Cameron pick your brain on a few business things."

Langsam's round eyes squished suspiciously. "What sort of business things?" he asked.

"Well," Cameron began uncertainly, "I've been charged with improving our company's customer experience. Maddy here suggested you might be able to give me a little insight." To what, he didn't add, he wasn't sure.

"Customer experience is what drives our business," Langsam said. His voice sounded harsh, almost angry. "It's the core of any organization. Everybody knows that. But I have neither the time nor the patience to educate other people on it."

"I'm curious," Cameron said, wondering if this man had any clue how bad his store was, "how is business?"

Langsam allowed himself a smug smile. "Business is great," he said. "Couldn't be better. Sales are down a little over last year, but our expenses are way down. Over the last two years, we've been able to cut our wage costs by over fifty percent, and with the introduction of cutting-edge technologies, we've done it without actually impacting our customer experience levels."

"You don't say?" Cameron said, fighting back a twitch. "That would be the automatic checkouts at the front of the store?"

"That's part of it," Langsam replied. "We also introduced a sophisticated CRM tool, telephone IVR system. Cut back on merchandising and other less relevant things. Focused on loss prevention. This place almost runs itself now, I tell you."

"IVR system?" Cameron asked.

"Interactive voice response system," came the pompous reply. "The computer does it all. It answers the phone, routes the calls. It's a lot more efficient than before, when we had to have people actually answer the phones."

"Really," Cameron said, trying to sound impressed.

"Really," Langsam said, again with a smug smile. "Look at this." He pulled a report from the pile on his desk. "Before we had our system, we were averaging forty calls a day. Now we're getting close to three hundred calls a day. Imagine how many more people we would have to employ to field that kind of volume. It was one of the best moves we've ever made."

"Are you sure the increase in calls isn't just the same people calling over and over again?" Cameron asked, thinking back to his earlier eavesdropping.

Langsam gave Cameron a sour look. "You're one of those guys who doesn't embrace technology, I see," he said. "But you're wrong. If that was the case, call escalations would be increasing instead of decreasing. In fact," he snatched another report from his desk, "we've had zero call escalations for the last three months."

"Have you thought that maybe people aren't just getting through, which is why they might be calling so frequently, and why they can't escalate calls?" Cameron said. "Isn't it possible you're actually losing money instead of saving money?"

Langsam's face darkened. "Do you have a problem?" he asked angrily. "Did you really come here to discuss customer experience, or were you just looking for an opportunity to disparage an operation of which you have no understanding?" He pounded one of his reports with his index finger. "It's really none of your business, *Mr. Household Solutions*, but I can tell you that if we were losing money, I would be the first to know about it."

"I'm really sorry," said Cameron, "I didn't mean to come across as negative. I'm just trying to understand."

Langsam glared at him impatiently. "Even if there ever was a problem with our telephone system, we have live chat," he said, oozing with contempt. "It's called *omni-channel customer service*. You should look it up sometime."

"Live chat? But you don't even have a website," Cameron said incredulously.

Langsam rolled his eyes. Cameron thought they might continue to roll right over the top of his head. "All websites do is give miscreants something to hack," he said as if it were the most obvious thing in the world. "We look after our customers, unlike Household Solutions."

Cameron was going to ask more about how they could have a live chat function without a website, but wasn't sure he wanted to hear the answer. Instead, he tried a different tact. "How often do you make it out into the store?" he asked. He had a hunch, which proved right.

"Been six years," Langsam said triumphantly. "This is a big ship, and I can't be doing everything. It runs better when we let people do what they do, without interference from me or the managers. Empowerment—that's what it's all about."

Cameron looked at Langsam's globe-like visage, wondering why Madeleine could have brought him here. "Wow, a ship that steers itself," he said. He tried to sound impressed.

Langsam glowered. "That's right. That's the way an organization should be run. Now is there anything else? I'm a busy man, and I don't have time to be educating people on Business 101."

"Actually," Cameron said unable to resist, "I am curious about your automatic checkouts. Are you aware that none of them are working?"

Langsam's eyes rolled together, and his eyebrows narrowed above them. "Don't be ridiculous!" he said scornfully. "Yes, I'm sure that, much to your delight, one or two are down occasionally, but to say none are working is just an attempt to provoke me. I don't know why you're so insistent in finding fault with our operations." He thumped his reports again with his finger. "Do you really think we'd be able to get this kind of performance with all of our automatic checkouts not functioning? I highly doubt it!

"Besides," he said to Cameron with an insipidly condescending smile, "we have a system where employees can help customers who are having difficulty with the cashes. So even if there were problems, we've got a back-up plan. It's called *Customer Service*." He drew the words out into a tone that seemed to tell Cameron he was too stupid to live.

Cameron fought to keep a stupefied expression from his face. *Is this guy for real?* Madeleine was digging in her purse for something. "But," Cameron said finally, "there are no customer service people out there."

Langsam's expression remained unchanged. "Of course not. Didn't you hear me when I told you we had streamlined the operation? It's called," he drew the words out slowly again, "*fiscal responsibility*." Langsam shook his head in wonder. He looked at Madeleine and sat back in his chair. "Household Solutions doesn't hire them very bright, do they?" he said to her. "No wonder they have such a bad reputation!

"Anyway," Langsam continued, half-standing again. "I really must ask you to leave. I have work to do, and you've given me a pounding headache." He wiped his dome theatrically, eyes rolling upwards.

Cameron stood. "I understand," he said, extending his arm to shake Langsam's hand. He did understand. He was getting a whopper himself. "Thanks for your time." Madeleine stood up as well. She pulled a long receipt and a pen out of her purse and handed them to Langsam.

"Just before we leave," she said cheerfully, "initial this, would you? I need to return a couple of bedding sets. Four hundred thread count indeed!"

Langsam looked like he was going to say something, then thought better. He initialed the receipt and handed it and the pen back to Madeleine. "Anything to get rid of you!" he grumbled.

They exited his office and began walking silently down the gray hallway. Cameron could again hear the ringing of the telephone. "Maddy," he asked finally. "Why did you take me here? This man knows nothing of customer experience. In fact, he's just plain scary. I'm not sure what I'm to learn from all this."

Madeleine smiled as she retraced her steps to the reception area. "I'm not sure what you'll learn from this, either," she said cryptically, "but I'd appreciate it if you'll let me know."

CHAPTER NINETEEN

THE FIRST THING CAMERON saw when he walked back to his office later that afternoon was another hand-written note on the top of his desk. He recognized the handwriting instantly as Gerard's. It only had five words on it.

Hi Cam—See me. Gerard.

Cameron punched the button to fire up his computer, grabbed a notepad from a desk drawer, and made his way to Gerard's office.

Gerard's desk and floor were piled with random stacks of papers and file folders. Cameron had a brief flashback to his visits to the Saggezza Centre. Behind the piles on his desk sat Gerard, leafing through the documents in a thick, red folder. He looked up when Cameron entered but didn't smile. *Uh-oh,* Cameron thought. *What now?*

"Have a seat Cam," Gerard said. "I'll be just a second." He went back to scanning the documents before him with an increasingly sour expression on his face. Cameron looked around for a place to sit. All of the chairs were covered in piles. Unsure what to do, he elected to just stand there. Just in case Gerard had some unseen system going, he didn't want to mess it up.

Gerard finished with his folder and set it to a stack on the floor to his right with a sigh. Obviously he hadn't found what he was looking for. "Oh, sorry Cam," he said when he saw Cameron still standing. "Just move those on to the floor."

Cameron gently moved the stack to an open spot beside the chair and sat down. "New filing system?" Cameron asked, nodding to the uncharacteristic clutter.

That brought a smile to Gerard's face, albeit a small one. "Welcome to my nightmare," he said, dropping back into his chair and clearing a pile between him and Cameron. "The IRS has graced me with an audit this year. I'm not that concerned about the outcome—I know better than to mess around with my taxes—but there's just a lot of documentation in a lot of random places. I just have to figure out where I put everything."

Cameron had never been audited before but had heard horror stories. "Sorry to hear that," he said. "I've never understood why they have to be so unreasonable when they do these things."

"Unfortunately," Gerard said with a sigh, "that's the part I do understand. It's really no different than when we audit our financial statements here at Household Solutions. If you don't look into the details, you don't learn the whole story. It's not really unreasonable, but it's not a lot of fun either." He looked up at Cameron. "Anyway, that's my problem. I wanted to find out how your problem is going."

"No such thing as problems boss—only lessons," Cameron said, repeating an oft-quoted Gerard-ism. Gerard smiled but didn't take his eyes off of Cameron. "In truth," Cameron said, "I'm starting to get some ideas. But I seem to be generating a lot more questions than I am answers at the moment."

"Timeline?" Gerard asked.

"Too soon to say," Cameron said truthfully. "But I'm hoping to at least have a handle on it within a couple of weeks." His insides squirmed a little. Two weeks might be wishful thinking.

"Good," Gerard said. "So you'll be presenting your plan to us at next Monday's meeting?"

"Monday?" Cameron started. "No, I meant two weeks from *today*."

Gerard's smile had vanished. "No can do, Cam," he said. "We've got to move on this while it's still fresh in everyone's minds. Besides, everyone's getting a little impatient. We need to show them we're making progress."

Humphries, Tremmel, and Tetu, Cameron thought. *Thanks for the pressure, guys.*

"But Gerard," he implored, "there's no point in making progress if we're not progressing in the right direction. I'm just not there yet. There's no way I can have a plan in place by Monday."

Gerard's voice made it clear the debate was over. "Sure you can," he said. "I have complete faith in you. Give it your best shot." He slid a pile in front of him and pulled out a sheaf of papers. "Now, if you'll excuse me, I have to resume my hunting." He looked at Cameron, who just sat their dumbly. "And I think you have a little work ahead of you, too."

Cameron took the hint, stood, and slowly walked out of Gerard's office. His insides felt tied in a knot. *Monday? What could he possibly have ready for Monday?* Back in his own office, he closed the door and dropped into his chair. He stared blankly at his monitor and considered his options.

A few minutes later, a knock on his door broke him from his thoughts. Without waiting to be invited, Stan Tetu stepped in and sat in Cameron's visitor's chair. "Hey Cam," he said with a smile, "sorry to bother you—I know you've got a lot on your plate—but I had an idea I thought I should float by you."

Cameron looked up and leaned back in his chair. "At this point, Stan," he said with a sigh, I'll take all the ideas you've got."

Tetu gave Cameron a brief, quizzical look, then continued. "I was looking at that new survey the JMB group had done. Theirs was pretty top-line, without a lot of detail, but it still made the point pretty well." Cameron nodded. "Well, I was thinking," Stan went on, "what if we dig a little deeper? And what if we track consumer attitudes towards our company on an ongoing basis, just as we're currently tracking their attitudes toward our products? I was thinking about it, because the new research sweep is scheduled to go out next week, and we could just piggy-back onto it. Actually," he handed Cameron a few loose pages, "I've already given some thought as to the types of questions we should ask."

Cameron looked down at the papers Tutu handed him and began to nod slowly. "Thanks, Stan." He was silent for a few more moments as something just below the threshold of consciousness struggled to get out.

"Thanks a lot," he said again appreciatively, with the beginnings of a smile forming on his face. "You may have actually helped me more than you know."

"How so?" Tetu asked.

"To be honest," Cameron said, "I'm not quite sure yet. I've just got a good feeling about this."

"Well, let me know soon," Tetu said, standing. "If we're going to make any changes, I have to let the market research company know ASAP." He was halfway out the door when he turned to Cameron. "Just out of curiosity, how are things going with the plan?"

Cameron thought for a moment. He had just spent the last two days wandering around a retail store with an eccentric old woman. How was he going to explain that?

"Slower than I thought. But I think things are starting to come together."

Tetu nodded. "Well, let me know if I can be of any help."

Cameron eyed him appraisingly. Maybe he'd been misreading him all this time. "I will, Stan. Thanks." With that, Tetu disappeared down the hallway.

Cameron looked down again at the pages. He felt a surge of energy as little pieces started falling together in his brain. *There's still something missing,* he thought, *but . . .*

On a hunch, he punched the speed dial for Vice President of Finance Will Abbott. Will picked up on the first ring.

"Hey, Will, it's Cameron. You got a minute?"

"Sure, Cam," Abbott replied, "What's up?"

"I'll be right over," Cameron said. "I just need to pick your brain a little." Cameron hung up and fairly sprinted to Abbott's office. On the way he passed by Gerard's office. The boss's head poked above the ever-growing stacks of documents. He didn't look happy.

In contrast, Will Abbott's office was clean and sparsely decorated. A simple, maple desk was surrounded by three, putty-colored, low credenzas. Two wall hangings—a picture of Abbot, his wife, and three young boys and the paper pronouncing him an official Chartered Accountant—were the only decorations in the room. Abbot's desk was completely clear except for a monitor, a plastic bottle of water, and a single file folder. Cameron mentally shook his head. He had never seen Abbott's desk any other way. He was the most organized man he had ever met.

If there was a picture in the dictionary beside the word accountant, it would be of Will Abbott. He was tall and lean with a thin face and thinning hair. His entire wardrobe seemed to consist of navy and gray pinstriped suits, plain white shirts, and blue and white, diagonally-striped ties. Beneath the bland and uninspiring exterior, however, was one of the brightest minds and nicest people Cameron knew. Cameron often kidded him about having way too many interpersonal skills to be an accountant.

A broad, welcoming smile spread across Abbot's face as Cameron leaned into his office. "Hi, Cam," he said. "That was fast. To what do I owe the honor?"

Cameron closed the door behind him, sat down, and leaned forward with his elbows on Abbot's desk. He allowed himself a small grin. In the few seconds it had taken him to span the distance from Gerard's office to here, an even larger number of the puzzle pieces had fallen into place with an almost audible thump. "Will," he said, looking at his watch, and then at the now-curious accountant, "it's 4:30. You've got half an hour to turn me into an accountant."

CHAPTER TWENTY

CAMERON HAD BEEN FRANTICALLY typing on the laptop on his dining room table for almost two hours when a sudden, sequential cascade of thoughts forced their way into his consciousness. An involuntary smile spread across his face. The first was the sudden understanding of Madeleine's cryptic comment about getting all the perspectives except the important ones. It had hit him like a slap in the forehead.

That thought triggered a growing understanding of exactly what he had to do to prepare for Monday's meeting. And this was followed by a realization of how much work he had to do between now and then. He was confident he could do it, but not if he had the distractions of the office around him. He nodded to himself. He would have to work from home.

Cameron took a sidelong glance at the only distraction he anticipated by working in the dining room. Chewbacca had gone back to investigate his invisible tormentor. He faced the wall, head cocked to one side, listening.

As Cameron mentally broke down the timelines, the next thought actually did make him slap his head. He realized with dismay that he was supposed to meet Madeleine the next morning at the Saggezza Center. There was no way he'd be able to do that now. He would have to call her right away to cancel.

He walked to the living room, picked up the telephone from the coffee table, and tapped in Madeleine's number. Madeleine answered it on the first ring.

"Oh, Cameron, I am SO glad you called. I meant to call you in your office earlier today, but I got so tied up trying to choose new paint for my den—well you know what that's like—anyway I settled on 'worn glove'—funny name for a paint, don't you think? Anyway, it's just going to look AMAZING. Well, then I was going to call you at home, but I started preparing chicken breast for dinner stuffed with honey, cranberry and Black Forest ham—oh it was so GOOD, you can't IMAGINE—but the point is it just completely slipped my mind that I told my sister in San Diego I would help her with some pity shopping—she has had SUCH a terrible time lately—anyway I really can't meet with you tomorrow—can we reschedule for Monday?"

Cameron was laughing out loud by the time she was finished. "No problem missing tomorrow, Maddy. Actually, that's why I was calling you. It looks like I have plans, too. Monday might not work, though. Got a big meeting. How's Tuesday?"

"Tuesday is perfect," Madeleine said. "So we'll see you then?"

"Actually, Maddy," Cameron said quickly before she could hang up, "do you have a minute? I've got something to run past you."

"Of course. Anything for you, Cameron!" Maddy said warmly. "What's up?"

"Well, for starters," Cameron began, "I know what perspective I was missing."

"Really!" Madeleine said. "Do tell!"

"It's the customer's," Cameron said. He waited for confirmation, but Madeleine said nothing. He continued. "The books I bought had some insight into general strategies—some of them very good—but they were all written by people who didn't know what it was like to be one of *our* customers. There is no way to apply the strategies, or to know which ones to apply, until I understand Household Solutions from our customers' perspectives.

"The senior management team was guilty of the same thing," Cameron continued. He was talking faster now. For the first time since undertaking this project, he was excited. "We were trying to come up with solutions before we really understood the issues as the customers see them."

"When you and I were walking through the Saggezza Center, we were getting the customer's perspective, and that's what made the difference. I had been wondering why Langsam had been so blind to the issues in the store, even though they were so apparent to me. But it's because *we* were the customers, and he hadn't been out in his store for six years."

He paused as another thought crashed through his consciousness. "And, just focusing on our customers isn't good enough. In order to fix things, we have to understand what it's like to *be* our customers."

"Go on," Madeleine encouraged.

"When we were in the office waiting room, you told me that customer experience wasn't a thing, but a perception. I get it now. And it's not just any perception. It's the customer's perception. In fact, when it comes to defining how good a company is at customer experience, there's really no one else's point of view that matters. What anyone else might think, including the senior management team at Household Solutions, is irrelevant. It doesn't matter what we're actually doing, or how good we might think we are. If the customer thinks we suck, then . . . well . . . we suck. Customer experience perception is customer experience reality."

"Perhaps not the words I would have chosen," Madeleine admonished with a smile in her voice. "But right nonetheless. So, Cameron, now that you've come to this epiphany, what's next?"

"Well, for starters, there's no point in doing anything—training, incentivizing, changing our operational focus—anything—until we get a better understanding of how our customers currently see us and what they really want from us. We can't change people's opinions if we don't know what they are."

"Hard to believe this is the same Cameron who three days ago thought shopping was a waste of time."

"Yeah, well, I'm a reformed man," Cameron said grinning. "Anyway, on that note, there's something else I want to talk to you about. I have a plan."

"How EXCITING!" Madeleine said encouragingly. "Well?"

Over the next ten minutes, he outlined his idea. Aside from a few "uh-huhs" and "okays," Madeleine stayed silent. "So?" he asked eagerly when he finished. "What do you think?"

"I think," Madeleine said cheerfully, "that I would love to be a fly on your boardroom wall on Monday!"

CHAPTER
TWENTY-ONE

AS THE SENIOR MANAGEMENT team filed into the boardroom, the first thing they saw was Cameron, sitting in his usual spot with a stack of folders in front of him. Attired in light khaki slacks and a navy blue golf shirt and sipping on a cup of fragrant coffee, Cameron looked anything but the part of corporate officer. He looked more like he had a date at a country club.

A few minutes after 8:00, Gerard appeared. He looked at Cameron. His eyebrow raised and the corners of his lips twitched a little, but he said nothing. A few minutes later, they were ready to get started.

Gerard stood and cleared his throat. "Well, folks," he began, "this is going to be the Cameron show today." All eyes turned to Cameron, who raised his coffee cup and nodded. Gerard continued. "To be fair, I should probably confess that I put a lot of pressure on him regarding this project." He gave Cameron a knowing smile. "I've asked him to have a plan together today and present it to you, but I think we all know he hasn't really had enough time to make it bulletproof. Even so, I need you to throw everything you've got at it. Anything that doesn't look right, say something." He nodded to Cameron, then walked over to sit beside Susan Tremmel. "Okay, Cam," he said. "Let's see what you've got."

Cameron stood, collected his folders, and went to the head of the table. Before he got started, Syd Rosen chirped up. "Are we keeping you from a golf game?"

Everyone laughed. Cameron grinned at him. "No, but you are cutting into my shopping time."

Syd pursed his lips. "Got you out of my department just in time," he observed in a stage whisper.

Cameron slid a folder across the table to each member of the senior management team. He powered on the LED screens behind him and looked around. "Everyone ready?" Nods around the table.

"I'd like to start by thanking everyone for your help and support," he began. "And for all of you who have already dedicated some of your valuable time to this." He smiled at Tremmel, Humphries, and Tetu. "What I've got to present this morning is, in fact, bulletproof." He shot a glance at Gerard, who was looking at him intently. "But I will ask for your indulgence and patience as I walk through it.

"The truth is, I don't really have any answers yet. In fact, I have a lot more unanswered questions today than I did a week ago. The good news, though, is that I've at least got a starting point. I know the types of questions that need to be asked, and where to ask the questions from."

"Where to ask the questions from?" Tetu asked.

"Exactly," Cameron acknowledged, but didn't elaborate on the point. "I have to admit I was struggling a little with this at first. I did a ton of research trying to figure out what we should do and how we should do it. The problem was that everyone seemed to have differing opinions. The books I read, the internet research I did . . . even in our small group, we each had a different take on how to tackle improving our customer experience." He looked again at Tremmel and Humphries. "And I'm sorry to hold up your initiatives. It's not that I don't think they're good ideas. I just want to make sure that we're taking the most effective approach before we jump into things."

To Cameron's relief, Tremmel and Humphries both nodded in agreement. Cameron continued. "I just think we need the answers to some questions before we begin. But not just any questions. We need the answers to the *right* questions. It's project management 101. The quality of a solution is directly proportionate to how well one defines the problem.

"It finally dawned on me that the reason I was having a hard time pinning down the answers was because, like the rest of us, I was asking the wrong questions. I'd been asking 'what should we do' and 'how should we do them' before I had the answers to 'why.'" Cameron didn't mention the part about Madeleine.

"Such as?" Gerard prompted.

"Well," Cameron responded, "the first question is, 'Why don't our customers like us?' I mean, the JMB Group gave us a little insight into that, but really nothing actionable. Stan has suggested that we should poll our customers to learn a little more about them and their attitudes toward us, which I think is a great idea." He nodded to Stan. "But I'm not even sure that goes deep enough. I think we really have to crawl inside our customers' brains and start seeing the world as they see it.

"We have to start asking ourselves questions from our customers' point of view. That's what I meant when I said we need to know where to ask the questions from. The fact is, these why questions are the ones our customers are already asking. Questions like, 'Why does Household Solutions do things the way they do?' or 'Why *don't* we do things a certain way?' They're asking these questions every day, and they're good questions. To be frank, they're questions we should have been asking ourselves a long time ago."

"What sort of why questions?" Gerard asked. The look in his eyes told Cameron he had captured his interest.

Cameron was ready for this. "That's the thing, Gerard. I don't know what they all are. I don't think any of us do. All I know is that they're out there, and they are a tremendous source of frustration to our customers. And I also know that, until we find what those questions are and can answer them adequately, we will never achieve the level of customer experience we're looking for."

"Can you give us any examples?" Syd asked curiously.

"Sure," said Cameron. "How about this one. Why do we make it so difficult for customers to make a legitimate warranty claim?"

Everyone looked at each other, puzzled. "What are you talking about?" Syd asked. "We don't make it difficult at all."

"Really?" Cameron said. "How do you know?"

"Because I would have heard about it," Syd said matter-of-factly. "Cameron, consumers are buying thousands of our products each day. If this was a problem, don't you think I'd have heard about it by now?"

"How would you have heard about it?" Cameron persisted.

"People would call, they'd write, they'd send emails, they'd open tickets," Syd said, looking around the table. "It would be on social media. People aren't shy about things like this. Am I wrong?" Everyone nodded in agreement and looked at Cameron.

Cameron looked back at them. He was surprised, but tried not to show it in his face. He thought of the constantly ringing telephone at the Saggezza Center and the pompous Langsam poking his report with his finger. He was prepared for the comment, although he had hoped it wouldn't come. He was a little surprised, though, that it had come from Syd—someone for whom he had an immense amount of respect.

Everyone was looking at him expectantly. Cameron nodded. "Okay," he said. "Let's play a game." He stepped to the corner of the room, and reached into one of the large cardboard boxes that had been sitting unobtrusively beside a long credenza. He began pulling out Household Solutions products, and handing them to the people seated around the table. When he was finished, he went back to the front of the room.

"Each of you now has one of our products in your hands. Each product is in a sealed box, exactly as our customers would buy it in a store." Cameron reached into his pocket, pulled out a fifty-dollar bill, and set it on the table. "I'd like you to pretend that the product you're holding is defective, and you're having challenges getting our warranty honored. This fifty," he said, "is for the first person who figures out how to successfully complain to us about it."

At first, everyone just sat there, looking at Cameron. *Was he serious?* Then they all started turning the boxes over in their hands, scanning them for contact information. Gerard reached into his pocket and pulled out a small Swiss Army knife and cut open the tape sealing his Auto-Baste Broiler. He pulled out the instruction manual and started leafing through it. Humphries reached over to borrow the knife, and did the same thing for her Xact-Portion Spice Dispenser. Soon, everyone around the table was flipping back and forth through their manuals. Syd pulled out his phone and began surfing the Household Solutions website. Two minutes later, he raised his fist in triumph. "Got it!" he exclaimed, reaching for the fifty. Cameron snatched it away before the COO's hand got to it.

"Not so fast!" Cameron warned. "What did you find?"

"Right here on our website," Syd said poking his phone, "under *Contact Us*, there's an address for warranty support."

"An address?" Gerard said. "No telephone number? No email address?"

"Nope," Syd began, "No, wait—I found a number, tucked away in the corner." He looked up at Cameron. "Now give me my fifty."

"Call the number first," said Cameron. "Then we'll see about the fifty."

Syd looked at him suspiciously. Cameron slid a telephone over to him. He'd been prepared for this, too. "Put it on speakerphone so we all can hear," he instructed Syd. Warily, Syd punched the numbers into the dial pad of the phone. One ring. Two rings. On the third ring, a friendly-sounding automated female voice came through the speaker.

"Thank you for calling Household Solutions, the world leader in household innovation. If you know the extension of the person you are calling, please dial or say the number now. To talk to a customer service representative, say 'customer service.'"

"Customer service," Syd said, leaning closer to the phone.

"I'm sorry," the friendly voice said, "I couldn't understand your response. Please try again."

"Customer service," Syd said again, this time a little slower and louder.

"I'm sorry," the friendly voice said, "I couldn't understand your response. Please try again."

Syd looked around the room. He rolled his eyes, rubbed his temples, and glanced at Cameron. "CUSTOMER SERVICE!" He said one more time, a lot louder.

There was a pause on the other end of the line. Finally the voice came back on saying, "I'm sorry you're having troubles. Please try again later." And the next thing everyone heard was a dial tone.

The room was silent. Gerard's face paled. Syd reached over and punched the disconnect button on the telephone. His usual pleasant demeanor was gone. He looked up at Cameron, then wordlessly, he hit the redial button.

"Thank you for calling Household Solutions, the world leader in household innovation . . ." the voice came on again, happy as ever. Syd punched the zero button, and the voice said, "I'm sorry, you have pushed an invalid extension. Please try again." Syd's face was red with frustration now. It was a sharp contrast to Gerard's. The blood had completely drained from his now, leaving it a pasty white.

"C-u-s-t-o-m-e-r S-e-r-v-i-c-e" Syd said, enunciating with comic slowness.

"Thank you," the cheerful voice said. "Let me connect you. Before I do, tell me, what product are you calling about?"

Syd buried his head in his hands and then looked up. "Follow-Me Track Light," he said, referring to the kitchen counter lighting system he had in front of him.

"I'm sorry," the cheerful woman said, "I'm not sure I understood your response. Did you say *vertical drop toaster*?"

Syd was angry now. "No, I did not!" he shouted at the telephone in the middle of the table. "I said, Follow-Me Track Light!'"

"I'm sorry," the voice said happily to a collective groan from the room, "I still didn't understood your response. Please wait, and I will get a customer service representative."

Syd looked around the room incredulously. Abbot actually slapped his forehead. Gerard sat frozen, staring at the telephone. Cameron picked up his mug and had a sip of coffee.

A moment later, a male voice came on the telephone. In contrast to the warmth of the computer voice, his was cool and disinterested. "Customer service, how may I help you?" he said.

"I'm having some problems with my Follow-Me Track Light. It doesn't seem to work," Syd said into the phone.

"What sort of problems?" the voice came back.

"It doesn't work," Syd repeated with annoyance. "What do I do to get a new one?"

"You should return it to the store you purchased it from, sir. They will look after it," the voice said flatly, without elaborating.

"I bought it two months ago, and the store won't take it back," Syd said. The entire senior management team was leaning forward on the boardroom table now in breathless silence. It was like listening to a train wreck.

"In that case, sir, you'll need to speak with our warranty support department." The disembodied voice actually sounded annoyed.

"O-kayyyy," Syd said slowly and deliberately, his frustration barely in check. "How would one go about doing that?"

"You just call the main number and say 'warranty support' at the voice prompt," the voice came back in a tone that suggested that this was something everyone knew.

"Thank you," Syd said with exaggerated politeness. "I don't suppose you could connect me?"

An irritated sigh came through the speaker. There was a click, a pause, and then, "Thank you for calling Household Solutions, the world leader in household innovation. If you know the extension of the person you are calling, please dial or say the number now. To talk to a customer service representative, say 'customer service' . . ."

Cameron had only ever seen the affable COO truly angry on two occasions in the entire ten years he had been at Household Solutions. This was the third, and it eclipsed the first two by a large margin. Rosen was standing now, face crimson, leaning over the telephone. "WARRANTY SUPPORT!" he shouted at it, daring it to disobey him.

There was a brief pause, and the happy woman's voice returned. "You have reached Household Solutions warranty support line. If your appliance requires repair or replacement, please return it to the store from which it was purchased. If it is past the store's return date, and within the product warranty date, please contact Household Solutions' customer service department at . . ." She recited the main number, thanked the caller, and then the line went dead. Syd pounded the disconnect button with his fist, silencing the dial tone, then fell back in his chair staring at the ceiling. There was a long pause while everyone just sat.

It was Cameron who broke the thick stillness. "Any questions?" he said quietly, reaching toward the center of the table, retrieving the fifty. Silent headshakes from around the room.

"Yeah, I've got one," Rosen muttered, still staring at the ceiling. "Are we almost done? I have to go down to our call center and kick some serious butt."

It was Gayle Humphries who spoke next. She was quiet and deliberate. "Cameron, what else have you found?" she asked.

"A few other things," Cameron admitted. "Equally disturbing. You don't even want to know about our live-chat process, or why we're not selling many molds for our Ice-Cream Cake Maker. I'd tell you about them, but I'm concerned about Syd's heart." Syd permitted himself a little smile, then resumed his glowering.

"The thing is," Cameron said, "we haven't been seeing these things because we haven't been looking at the world from our customer's perspective. And there's no way we can even begin to fix our problem until we have a better idea of what it's like to be Household Solutions customers. We need to start asking ourselves the same questions our customers are asking us—the why questions—then work our way back from there."

Cameron turned to Gerard. The CEO had barely moved since the warranty support demonstration. There was a fire in his eyes. "Gerard, when you first asked me to take this on, you asked me to estimate how much money we were losing because of our customer experience levels. Do you remember the number we came up with?"

"Thirty-six million dollars," Gerard said without hesitation. "A hard number to forget."

"Yes, well, about that," Cameron said, pausing for effect.

"Based on just the little I've seen so far, I think that number might be wishful thinking." Eyes looked around the table, then back at Cameron. No one spoke. No one doubted him.

"The good news is that it's fixable," Cameron said, reaching toward folder in front of him. "I don't know how to fix it yet, but it's only logical to assume that since we've gotten ourselves into this mess we can get ourselves out of it. To do this, though, I'm going to need help from all of you. And I'm going to need a lot of your time. I know how busy you all are, but I can't see any other way to do it."

"Anyone too busy to help out?" Gerard asked without looking around. It wasn't really a question, but everyone shook their heads anyway. "Good," he said soberly, turning to face Cameron. "What's the plan, Cam?"

"Well, it was actually you who gave me the idea," Cameron said to Gerard. The CEO raised an eyebrow. Cameron looked back at him with a wry smile. "Sorry, boss, but you're in for another audit."

CHAPTER TWENTY-TWO

"OH, MY DAY JUST keeps getting better," Gerard growled. "An audit?"

"A customer experience audit," Cameron responded. "With some help from Will, here," he indicated Will Abbott who had been observing silently, "I think I've come up with a way for us to get a look at how customers view our company."

He flipped open his folder. "A variation of the audit process seemed to be the right way to go," he continued. "In the simplest terminology, the purpose of any audit is to prove things. In our company financials, for example, we make certain assertions as to our financial position. We claim to have generated specific income, and to have incurred specific expenses against that income. An audit is the process we use to test each of these assertions for validity. The audit seeks to prove or confirm each item."

"What I'm proposing is that we do the very same thing with all of the customer touch-points in our company. But instead of trying to prove the validity of things from a financial point of view, I want to prove the validity of everything from a customer experience point of view." Cameron looked around the room and saw heads nodding. He was happy to see that this included Syd.

"I'd like to take a look at every nook and cranny; every process and policy. I want to look at the validity of each—not from an efficiency or cost effectiveness point of view as we have in the past—but from the customer's perspective. It's not that efficiency and effectiveness aren't important—don't get me wrong. I'm an engineer after all, and goodness knows these things are near to my heart. But I think until we can weigh them against their effect on the customers, we can't really make sound decisions as to the right things to do.

"At first, I was considering hiring an outside company like the JMB Group to do the audit. And I still might once we get going. But I think we have to get on this quickly, and it occurred to me that we all might benefit by being directly involved. We all know the company well and can access things without jumping through a lot of hoops."

It was Gayle Humphries' turn to speak up. "But how can we be objective?" she asked. "Let's face it. As you pointed out, we're the ones who've put ourselves in this position in the first place!"

"True," Cameron said nodding. "There's no way we could effectively or objectively look into our own silos. So, what I've done is assign you each a specific area that is not under your responsibility. If I could get you to open your folders, you'll see your assignments." Everyone reached for their folders and began scanning the contents.

"I haven't had time to make comprehensive lists of criteria, so I'm hoping each of you will build on these. Use them as a starting point. Here's who's got what: Stan, you're going to look into all the financial operations. Susan, you're going to dig into our sales and marketing practices. Will, you've got HR. Gayle—production, supply chain, and logistics.

"What about me?" Syd asked, holding up his folder. "My folder just has one word in it—'customer.' What does that mean?"

Gerard then held his folder up. "Me too," he said.

Cameron smiled at them and held up his finger as if to ask for one more moment. "Yours is the most important. But before I get to it, I want to make sure everyone else understands what I'm asking."

"If I read this right," Humphries said, indicating her folder, "you want me to dig through all of our production and logistics policies and procedures, and think about them from a customer's point of view. Is that about it?"

"Precisely," Cameron said. "It means you'll have to spend time on the floor, talking with shippers and receivers; reviewing our inventory control procedures; looking at our manufacturing practices, etcetera—and assessing how each of these impact our customers."

Humphries nodded.

Will spoke up next. "Cam," he said, a slightly puzzled look on his face. "You've got me looking into HR, which is fine . . . but I'm not exactly sure how our HR practices impact our customers."

"Perhaps they don't," Cameron admitted, "but as you told me when you were educating me about audits—if you don't look, you won't find."

Will nodded, and looked from his folder to Cameron with a wry grin. "Touché," he said.

"I also think," Cameron said after a moment, "that we will find out things about our internal customer experience as well— and that it might prove to be just as important as the experience our external customers have." Nods around the room.

"Folks, this is going to be difficult," he said solemnly to the group. "You're going to be sticking your nose into each other's business, and very possibly coming up with a lot of things that require improvement. In order for this to work, we can't be afraid of hurting each other's feelings. More importantly, you can't allow your feelings to get hurt when someone starts asking hard questions about policies and procedures that might be near and dear to you. As of right now, nothing is sacred. Let's all work on the assumption that everyone has the company's best interests at heart, and that everything about our business might be changing." More nods.

He gestured toward the CEO and COO. "Syd and Gerard are going to be both your sounding boards and the advocates of the customers. Their job is going to be to look at Household Solutions from our customers' points of view."

"How do we do that?" Rosen asked, uncertainly.

"By being customers," Cameron answered. "Syd, you're going to call up a dozen or so of our biggest commercial customers—retailers, wholesalers, distributors, etcetera, and arrange to be a fly on the wall of their operations. You're going to sit in their offices, talk to their buyers and their executives. You're going to watch them interact with us and other suppliers. You're going to hear the 'why' questions first-hand."

"That's going to require pulling in a lot of favors," Syd observed. "I'm not sure that our customers will be all that keen at letting us embed that deeply into their organizations."

Cameron nodded. "You're probably right," he said. Then he smiled. "Fortunately, with your sparkling charm and charisma, this shouldn't be too much of a challenge." Syd looked at Cameron and rolled his eyes.

Cameron turned next to Gerard. "Gerard, you're going to spend the next two weeks visiting our retailers and our e-commerce site. You're going to be an end user, buying things, reading instructions, trying to return things, asking questions, trying to connect with us. You're going to be the voice of the everyday consumer.

"What I would like both of you to do is report in regularly to the person responsible for investigating each area. So, for example, Syd, if you hear people complaining about a certain aspect of product delivery, pass the comments on to Gayle to investigate what's causing the issue. Gerard, if you hear someone complaining that a product isn't living up to its billing, pass that on to Susan."

Cameron looked at the rest of the group. "As for everyone else, whenever you see something that you think might be adversely affecting customers, give Gerard or Syd a call to get the take from their end. That will serve to validate your concerns and give insight into what areas to delve a little deeper in."

Cameron looked around the room. "Any questions?" he asked.

"Timelines?" Abbott responded.

"Oh, right!" Cameron said, looking at his notes, then back up at the senior management team. "You've got two weeks from today. After that we're going to share our results, come up with a plan, and get to work."

"Two weeks!" Tetu exclaimed. "A little tight, don't you think?"

"It is," Cameron agreed. The corners of his lips twitched. "If you want an extension, just ask Gerard." One quick look at the CEO's face told everyone that wasn't going to happen.

"I have a question," Rosen grumbled, eying Cameron.

"Shoot," Cameron said.

"What are you going to be doing while we're all working our butts off?"

Cameron hesitated and thought of Madeleine. He smiled at the COO. "Well, I'm not really sure. But I think I have some shopping to do."

CHAPTER TWENTY-THREE

THE MORNING WAS WARM and sunny. A persistent light breeze from the ocean had temporarily pushed away the smog that usually blanketed Los Angeles, and the sun took full advantage, brightening everything it touched. Even the street vendors' faded umbrellas seemed to regain some of their luster.

Cameron stood outside the Saggezza Center soaking it in. He wondered what Madeleine had in store for him today. This morning, he hadn't even bothered to bring his portfolio. He'd pretty much given up on the idea of asking Madeleine what she was charging him, or trying to prepare a statement of work, or any of the more formal things one might do with a consultant. He was just going to see where he ended up.

A flash of bright white caught the corner of his eye, and he smiled. It was Madeleine, dressed in a white pants suit and white top. The only color she wore was a royal blue belt to match the band around her white fedora. Her hair was streaked pecan-blonde. *Does she do her hair every day,* Cameron wondered?

She strode purposefully through the milling crowd, looking about her like a queen overseeing her domain. She smiled when she saw Cameron. Reaching him, she stopped, placed both hands on her hips and looked at him appraisingly. "Well," she said, "aren't we casual today!"

Cameron grinned. He had forgone his business casual attire for a pair of navy slacks with a white-and-blue golf shirt. "I figured that if I was going shopping there was no need to dress up." He stepped back and gave Madeleine a quick approving once-over. "But apparently, I was wrong."

"Oh, pish," Madeleine said, rolling her eyes theatrically, "these old things?" She extended her arm toward the Saggezza Center door. "Shall we?"

"We shall," Cameron said, taking her arm and leading the way into the store.

As they entered into the lobby, Cameron instinctively began walking toward the discreet doors on the left that housed the elevators. Madeleine, however, kept walking straight ahead into the store in front of them. When she saw the direction Cameron was heading, she stopped and asked, "Where are you going?"

Cameron looked at her, "Oh, I just assumed . . ." he began.

"Still making assumptions?" Madeleine sighed. "Ah, well. And I had such high hopes for you too . . ." Her eyes met Cameron's and twinkled as she turned to resume her walk into the first level store. "You've graduated, young man!" she proclaimed. "It's time to move on!"

As they entered, Cameron instantly saw the difference between this and the basement store the previous week. The aisles were clean, the shelves were full, and merchandise was priced. It was brightly lit, and people all around were pushing large, new shopping carts.

"Well, this is a welcome change," Cameron said to Madeleine as they stood looking at the store. "I'll bet they do a lot better than the store in the basement."

"Indeed," Madeleine agreed, "although there is something even more important about this store that you should know."

"What's that?" asked Cameron.

Madeleine turned to him, her eyes positively glowing. "It's their annual spring blow-out sale!" she said excitedly. "Thirty percent off all women's wear! Lingerie forty percent off! Now until Friday only! Best deals in town!" She sounded like an infomercial.

She danced over to a bank of shopping carts Cameron hadn't noticed. "Care to join me?" she asked.

"Er," Cameron said hesitantly. "I think I'll just poke around a bit myself. I, uh, wouldn't want to . . ." He pondered the nicest way to say it. "Slow you down."

"Well, that's *very* considerate of you!" Madeleine smiled at him sweetly. "Shall we meet at the checkouts in, say, forty minutes?"

"Deal," said Cameron. And with that, Madeleine positioned herself behind her cart and marched away.

Standing alone, Cameron looked around trying to decide where to begin. Eventually, he elected for a methodical, aisle-by-aisle approach. As he wandered down the first row, he was struck again by how much better run this store seemed. The shelves were lower, with merchandise more accessible. The signs and prices were clear, the aisles were open. This company was obviously paying attention to its presence, and had put some pretty effective processes in place.

One oddity he did notice were bright orange signs appearing from the shelves every eight feet or so. In bold, black type, they proclaimed: *IF YOU BREAK IT, YOU'VE BOUGHT IT.* He had, of course, seen this type of sign before—usually in smaller boutiques and generally couched in cute poetry like, *Lovely to look at, lovely to hold, but if you break it, consider it sold.* For some reason they always rubbed him the wrong way, although he couldn't put his finger on why.

Cameron continued his journey around the store. More of the good merchandising and layout, and more of the signs. Occasionally the *IF YOU BREAK IT, YOU'VE BOUGHT IT* signs were interspersed with other signs in white type on black background. *NO REFUNDS. EXCHANGE OR CREDIT NOTE ONLY.* He also saw more than one angry-looking sign warning would-be thieves that *STORE POLICY: SHOPLIFTERS WILL BE PROSECUTED.*

Funny, Cameron thought. Even though this floor was much better organized, in some ways he actually felt more uncomfortable. Almost like he was unwanted. He wandered into the kitchenware section, and began scanning the shelves for

Household Solutions products.

As he was letting this sink in, a fifty-something couple came down the aisle and stopped in front of the Rechargeable Counter Scrubbers. "These things are great!" the husband said to his wife, picking up a box and examining it. "Joey would like one of these." He pointed at the picture on the box. "But see the rotating brush there?" he said to her, "It works fine up until you get to a corner, then the brush is too wide. What they need is a couple of different sizes and shapes to get into corners and things. After all, that's where the dirt can really pile up."

It was all Cameron could do to resist saying, "Hey, great idea!" Instead he just pretended to be engrossed in the selection of toasters.

"So you should call them," the man's wife said. "It sounds like a good idea. I'm sure they'd appreciate it."

"You'd think so, wouldn't you," the man snorted. "I did call them a couple of months ago. Spent ten minutes navigating their telephone system to finally get an operator. I asked for a name or number of someone in product design, and she said that it was against their policy to give out people's names and numbers. God forbid, I guess, that someone might actually talk with a customer."

"So, what did you do?" the woman asked.

"Nothing," the man replied with a shrug. "Why should I care more than they do?" He turned his head as a thought struck him. "But maybe I'll give a call to their competition. Maybe they'd appreciate a good idea"

Cameron closed his eyes and waited for a wave of nausea to pass. He considered introducing himself to the couple, but decided against it, remembering the last time he had told someone where he worked. He turned and slowly walked away from them. *How was it that all these things were happening with no-one at Household Solutions realizing it?* he asked himself for the hundredth time. He looked down at his shoes while he walked. The last week or so had given him the answer to that question, of course. But it didn't make him feel any less stupid. He wondered if they were really going to be able to fix all this.

CHAPTER
TWENTY-FOUR

CAMERON STOOD IN FRONT of the checkout counters waiting for Madeleine. He'd spent the last forty minutes wandering through all of the aisles in the store and was impressed with the obvious attention to detail in the store operations. The store was clean, tidy, well-merchandised, brightly lit and well-stocked with clearly priced products. The merchandise was accessible and appropriate for the season. Cameron wasn't an expert in retail operations, but he knew this hadn't happened by accident.

One of the other things he noticed was that, like Langsam's basement store, there were no employees visible except for at the cash area. More than once, he'd seen customers looking around in vain for help, then abandoning their quest. He guessed that a half-dozen customer service people in the store would pay for themselves in incremental sales many times over.

Unlike Langsam's store, however, this one actually did have some people at the checkouts. There were seven in total. Five had cashiers, and two were the same self-serve checkouts he had seen earlier. These automated cashes seemed to be working, although each had large signs outlining what customers were and weren't allowed to do.

The live cashiers at the other checkouts could have been clones of the gray, zombie-like woman in the store below them. Although they didn't have the long lines, they were just as expressionless and interminably slow. As he looked around, he suddenly realized all the shoppers—or so it seemed—had Household Solutions Pressure Blenders in their carts. Some, in fact, had two or three. *Wow,* he thought, *Stan must have some marketing initiative out I'm not aware of. It sure is working.*

He walked a closer to the line in time to see a twenty-something woman with long black hair take a Pressure Blender out of her basket and hand it to the cashier. The price that appeared on the small LCD screen over the register was $10.99. He looked twice to make sure. Could that be right? He knew what that most stores retailed it for $109.99. It dawned on him that this was a glitch in the store's point-of-sale system. Somehow the wrong price had been inputted and people found out. He wondered how long the glitch had been there. He made a mental note to tell someone about it.

Cameron was so enthralled with this new development he didn't hear the sound of an approaching shopping cart. He started when Madeleine's cheerful voice came behind him. "I am SO sorry I took so long," she said. "But who KNEW they would have all the latest spring fashions in ALREADY!" She began pulling things from her stuffed cart. "And the PRICES! OmiGOSH!"

Cameron suppressed a smile as she displayed her items one at a time with a detailed color commentary on their price and quality. When she got to the lingerie layer of her shopping, he put his hand up. "Okay!" he said with a laugh. "We're getting into the 'way too much information' area here."

Madeleine looked at him reproachfully. "Oh pish," she said "You are SO old-fashioned!"

"Perhaps," Cameron said with a grin, "but I'll make it up to you." He leaned forward conspiratorially. "I've also discovered the deal of the century!" he stage whispered.

Madeleine cocked her head and looked at him expectantly. "Do tell," she said.

Cameron told her about the glitch in the system he'd witnessed. "They are selling it for a fraction of what it cost them," he said. "Obviously word has gotten out, so I'm guessing this has been happening for a while now."

"Indeed," Madeleine agreed. "I would think it's been at least six months." Cameron turned to look at his companion. Her eyes were twinkling. He raised one eyebrow and waited.

Madeleine shrugged. "I bought six of them in November to give away as Christmas presents," she confessed. Cameron nodded resignedly. So much for his grand discovery.

The person in front of them finished paying, and Madeleine pushed the cart to the cash and began unloading forty minutes of power-shopping. The cashier scanned them in slowly while Cameron and Madeleine looked on. When she came to the last item, a cream-colored cashmere sweater, she held it up and said emotionlessly, "This is part of a set. There should be a skirt that goes with it." Her lifeless eyes looked at Cameron, as if to say, "Well?"

"Heavens!" Madeleine exclaimed, "I must have left it on a shelf. I'll run and get it." She spun and speed-walked in the direction of the women's clothing department.

"Six fifty-two fifty three," the cashier said to Cameron.

"What?" Cameron asked, turning back to the cashier. She indicated the amount showing on the cash register screen. "Six fifty-two fifty three," she repeated.

"Oh . . . I . . ." Cameron began, then realized that the woman didn't care that it wasn't his merchandise. He sighed, reached into his wallet, extracted a credit card, and handed it to her. "This card has had quite a workout over the last little while," he said. If the cashier heard him, she gave no indication. She slid the receipt and pen over to Cameron to sign. He did and handed it back.

As if on cue, Madeleine appeared beside him. She waved a cream-colored cashmere skirt at the cashier, and placed it in a bag with the sweater. "Well THAT was a close one!" she said.

"Indeed," Cameron deadpanned. "If you'd gotten back any sooner, you'd have had to paid for all of this."

Madeleine laughed. "You are TOO funny!" she said. "Now, back to work. There's someone I think you should meet."

Cameron followed Madeleine as she turned to the left and toward the door to the store office. When they got there,

Cameron could see the sign beside the door: *Absolutely no soliciting, trespassers will be prosecuted, no money is kept on premises, no meetings without appointments, all visitors must have two forms of identification, dress code in effect.* Cameron grimaced and opened the door for Madeleine.

The reception area was clean and brightly lit. Its sparse appointments included four straight-back, wooden chairs and a small end table with three magazines on it. The receptionist sat behind a gray steel desk looking like a schoolteacher transported from the 1800s. Straight-backed with auburn hair pulled back in a severe bun, she wore a no-nonsense, high-necked frock in black and a stern face. She turned as they entered and eyed Madeleine, Cameron, and the shopping cart with a sour look.

"May I help you?" came a clipped, haughty voice. Under her gaze, Cameron had the distinct feeling that he'd done something wrong.

"I'm sure you may!" Madeleine said sweetly. "We're here to see Mr. Normas."

"Do you have an appointment?" came the cool response.

"I'm sure we must," Madeleine said. "After all, we do have to have an appointment to see people, now don't we?" She gestured to a replica of the door sign that was mounted on the front of the desk.

The receptionist arched an eyebrow and looked down at the screen in front of her. "Your name?" she inquired.

Now it was Madeleine's turn to raise her eyebrows. Still smiling, she tilted her head down and locked her gaze with the receptionist over the top of her glasses. "Really," she asked, "must we go through this one again?" While the smile was on her face, it was definitely not in her voice.

Cameron thought he saw a brief flinch on the part of the receptionist, but she held her ground. She broke eye contact with Madeleine and looked down at her screen. A moment later she looked back up with an air of quiet defiance. "I have no notes regarding an appointment for Mr. Normas at this time," she said stonily. "And I can't let you in without an appointment. That is a clearly indicated policy."

"And a good one it is, too!" Madeleine exclaimed, suddenly

brightening. "Otherwise people would be just wandering about willy-nilly! She leaned forward and looked upside down at the monitor. "So there's no appointment listed in there for Mr. Normas right now?" she asked incredulously.

"None whatsoever," the receptionist said smugly.

"Wonderful!" said Madeleine with a pleased look. "That means we won't be interrupting him in the middle of a meeting. He's a very important man, you know!" She reached over the counter and pushed a small, black button beside the computer monitor. The receptionist let out a flustered cry and began waving her arms about. Cameron heard the buzzing sound of the door to the inner offices unlocking. "Come along," Madeleine said to Cameron. "We mustn't keep Mr. Normas waiting!" She took his arm and led him through the door. Turning to the agitated receptionist just before the door closed behind them, Madeleine smiled and indicated the shopping cart they'd left beside her desk. "Oh, be a dear, would you, and keep an eye on my things for me?"

Madeleine scrupulously ignored the "Stop! You can't go in there! I'm calling security!" coming from the reception area as they walked down the hallway.

Cameron gave his companion an appraising look as they walked. "You don't take no for an answer, do you?" he said.

Madeleine looked at him in surprise. "And why should I?" she asked.

Cameron grinned. "The customer is always right, is that it?" he said.

"Oh, pish," Madeleine scoffed, "The customer is not always right, and you know it." She raised a finger and looked at him. "But the customer *is* always the customer," she said, "and 'no' is really *such* an offensive word, don't you think?"

"Offensive?" Cameron said with a smile. "I've never thought of it as being offensive before."

"But it is," Madeleine insisted. "Nothing good ever comes from saying no to a customer."

"Well, wait a minute," Cameron objected. "Don't you sometimes have to? I mean, sometimes you just can't give a customer what they want."

"Perhaps," Madeleine said, "but that's no excuse for not trying to give them what they need, is it?"

Cameron was thinking about this comment for a moment when they came to a stop at the end of the hallway. In front of them was a large wooden door with 'N.L. Normas, General Manager' on a simple brass plaque. Madeleine knocked softly, then turned the handle and walked in.

The man seated behind the desk was expecting them, obviously having been warned by the receptionist. He didn't speak, but there was an unmistakable look on his face asking them to explain themselves.

Normas' light-gray flannel suit had been pressed to an inch of its life but still looked unstructured over his thin, taut frame. His close-cropped, graying brush cut and long, drawn face gave him the no-nonsense look that Cameron always associated with ex-military brass. He was clearly someone who liked to be in control and was used to getting his own way. Madeleine, in typical fashion, ignored his intimidating demeanor.

"Thank you SO much for agreeing to see us on such short notice!" she said effusively. "I know what a busy man you are. I'm positively HONORED!"

He doesn't look busy, Cameron thought. The desk had a monitor, a keyboard and one lone sheet of paper on it, squared exactly to the desktop. A simple ballpoint pen paralleled it on the right.

"I *am* quite busy," Normas confirmed coldly. "And you don't have an appointment."

"Don't be silly!" Madeleine exclaimed. "I must have an appointment, or I wouldn't be here now, would I?" The man behind the desk blinked twice in a brief moment of confusion. She continued before he could say anything. "My friend, Cameron here, is with Household Solutions. He was hoping to learn a little from you about customer experience."

Normas didn't acknowledge Cameron and kept a steady eye on Madeleine. "I would, of course, be more than pleased to cooperate," he said flatly, "but we do have a clear policy in place for arranging such informational sessions. It involves completing the requisite request forms and non-disclosure agreements." He tilted his head and gave them both a contemptuous look. "Oh," he continued with unconcealed sarcasm, "and it also involves . . . an *appointment*."

Cameron couldn't remember the last person he had taken such an instant disliking to. He looked at Normas sitting silently at his desk with his hands folded in front of him. Arrogance just seemed to ooze out of him. Cameron couldn't resist. "Is there a purpose behind all this formality, or does it just make you feel good?"

If Normas recognized this as a return volley of sarcasm, he gave no indication. "There is indeed a purpose," he said smugly. "One which I could share with you if you were, in fact, supposed to be here." He looked squarely at Cameron. It was clear that he had no intention of providing any assistance.

After a few moments of silence, Cameron turned to Madeleine. "He's quite rude, isn't he?" he said to her as if Normas wasn't there.

"He is," Madeleine agreed.

"Did you bring me here for a reason?" he asked.

"I did," Madeleine said.

"Is there any point to us staying here?" he asked her.

"None that I can think of," Madeleine answered.

"Should we be polite and say goodbye, or should we just leave?" Cameron asked, still ignoring the GM.

"Oh, we can't do that!" Madeleine admonished. "Then it would be we who were the rude ones."

Cameron nodded and turned to Normas. "Goodbye," he said. Normas didn't respond.

Madeleine leaned toward the desk with a sweet smile. "Goodbye," she echoed. She reached out and gently nudged the piece of paper sitting on the GM's desk so that it was no longer perfectly aligned. Cameron thought he saw the man's eye twitch.

On the way out the door, Cameron turned to get one last look at the officious man. Sure enough, he was reaching for his paper, readjusting it so that it again sat square on the desk.

"Why on earth did you take me to see this man?" Cameron asked as they walked away from the office.

Madeleine looked at him quizzically. "Why, so you could learn something about customer experience, of course. Isn't that what we're supposed to be doing?"

"But he had nothing to offer!" Cameron exclaimed. "You must have seen this coming. He is so arrogant—with all his rules and processes and procedures. Customer experience isn't even on his radar!"

"That's true," Madeleine admitted with a wry smile. "He is quite confident in the way he does business, isn't he? But surely you must have learned something from him?"

"Yeah," Cameron grunted, "I learned I don't like him. But I'm not sure there was much of a customer experience lesson there."

"Really," Madeleine said plainly. "Hmm. Pity."

Cameron felt a familiar tug in his stomach. He was being set up again and he knew it. They walked down the hall in silence until they came back to the reception area door. Just as Cameron reached to open it, Madeleine spoke.

"I'm a wee bit curious as to why you didn't tell Mr. Normas about that little pricing glitch in their system," she said innocently. "After all, it must be costing them a lot of money, and it would have been a nice gesture."

Cameron made a face. "Why on earth would I want to do that?" he asked incredulously. "I mean, I had actually fully intended to, but after the way he treated us, why would I want to help him out? Heck, I'm half-tempted to buy all the products he's got, then turn around and sell them back to him! We'd still make a hefty profit."

Madeleine's eyebrows rose. "Gracious," she said. "Aren't we in an uncharitable mood this morning!"

"I'm not uncharitable," Cameron said defensively. "But he obviously doesn't care about me. Why should I care about him?"

"Good point," Madeleine said as she opened the door. "No reason at all, I guess." Then with mock disappointment, she added, "Too bad there's no customer experience lesson here."

Cameron stopped and stared at her as their conversation sunk in. She turned and looked at him with an innocent expression.

"You really enjoy it when I say stupid things, don't you?" he said finally.

Madeleine thought about this for a moment. "Yes," she said finally with a big smile. "Yes I do."

CHAPTER
TWENTY-FIVE

CAMERON WALKED INTO THE boardroom fifteen minutes before the meeting was to begin, surprised to see everyone else already there. Unlike the usual atmosphere, however, today was decidedly not collegial. Susan Tremmel and Stan Tutu were having a heated argument at the table. Stan was obviously on the attack, and Susan kept shrugging and shaking her head. Will Abbott was listening in and every now and then pointing an angry finger at Stan. Standing off in the corner, Gerard, Syd, and Gayle were in deep discussion.

Cameron made his way to the front of the room and set his coffee down on a coaster. He stood watching the interplay for a few moments. He had been half-expecting this. The deluge of emails that had flown around over the last week had grown increasingly more confrontational. He'd even caught himself almost sending off a terse email to Gayle regarding some of the pointed questions she had been asking at one of the manufacturing facilities. He had been pretty confident that this was going to be an interesting meeting. Raising his coffee mug, he called things to order.

"Hi, folks," he said. The conversation gradually died down as the leadership team turned their attention to him.

"So, you're one week into your two-week mandate," he said. "Nice to see everyone getting along so well." Not even a flicker of a smile in the room. *Uh oh*, Cameron thought.

"Well then, let's see where we are." He turned to the CEO. "Gerard, you've been the eyes of the end consumer. Why don't you start?"

Gerard didn't bother to stand. His usual effusive, confident tone was gone. He sounded tired. "I'm not sure where to start," he began. "I visited ten retailers around LA and bought twelve products. I learned that Household Solutions doesn't stand by their products, doesn't carry stock of accessories, and when we do we ship, we send the wrong products to customers. People can't easily get through to us, and when they do, they're treated like inconveniences."

"As to the 'why' questions Cameron spoke about, they include the ones we found out about last week. Why is it so hard to get through to warranty support? Why do we advertise color options on our packaging when there is only one color available? Why don't we have on our website an updated list of retailers who carry our products? Why are the people in our call center so rude?" Gerard paused for a moment on that one, and turned to Syd. "I'm serious. There's a Rachel in our call center who I'm going to hunt down and fire personally. And when I find out who hired Daniel, there's going to be some serious conversations happening there, too," he said.

"One of the big questions is why our retailers and our own people don't know more about our products. I talked with one or two CSRs who seemed to know what they are talking about, but most were just making stuff up as they went along." He looked at Human Resources VP Susan Tremmel and Marketing VP Stan Tetu. "Do we not train anyone? Do we not send out product information? Do we not have a knowledge base?" Cameron could see both colleagues tense up, but neither responded to the CEO's rhetorical question.

"I spent my evenings on householdsolutionssucks.com, and deathtohouseholdsolutions.com reading as many of the 400-

plus posts as I could stomach," Gerard continued, obviously agitated. "Do you know how many people tried to send me emails complaining about us?" He looked around the room. No one ventured a guess. "ME NEITHER! Because I never received any of them! But if only a fraction of the people posting were telling the truth, I should have received hundreds—maybe thousands!"

He turned back to Syd. "Do *you* know where these emails are ending up?" Syd shook his head. "Does anyone?" Gerard persisted, looking again at his team." If anyone knew, they weren't talking. Cameron again had a vision of the unanswered telephone at the Saggezza Center. He imagined some computer in the bowels of the Household Solutions building with a hard disk bloated with unanswered emails, ready to explode. "Why the hell didn't we see this earlier?" Gerard demanded in a loud voice to no one in particular. A thick silence filled the room.

"Because we weren't looking," Cameron finally responded. Everyone shifted their attention to him.

"You said it yourself, Gerard," Cameron said quietly, "in our first meeting on this. You said you were afraid we had been oblivious to these types of things, and that's why you called JMB."

Cameron stood and scanned the serious faces around the table. His soft voice contrasted with the stark reality of his words. "We're no different than anyone else out there, really. Every organization has opportunities to improve. But we got complacent. We became so convinced of our own awesomeness that we lost touch with the only people who really matter—our customers." Silent nods around the room.

"You want to know what our problem is, in one simple sentence?" Cameron asked. Gerard's eyes rose to meet his. "We just don't care about our customers. All we want is their money. It's as simple as that."

The room erupted. It was as if all of the frustration of the last week suddenly crystalized and focused on Cameron. "That is absolutely unfair and uncalled for!" CFO Gayle Humphries shouted angrily over the others. "We may have been making mistakes, but there's not a single person around this table who can be accused of not *caring*." Agreement echoed around the room.

Cameron waited for the voices around him to die down, then said to Humphries, "Really Gayle? Where's the evidence?" He continued before she could answer. "We've invested our time, efforts, and money on trying to become more innovative and more efficient. And even more time and money on branding, marketing, and advertising. But where has the investment been on improving our connection with the people who buy our products?"

He turned to Susan Tremmel. "Susan," he asked, "in round numbers, how much was your budget for things related to customer experience this year—training, coaching, onboarding, etcetera?"

Susan's shoulders rose subconsciously as she tried to recall her budget numbers. "Hard to say exactly," she said slowly. "It's not like we have a budget line that says 'Customer Experience HR Stuff.' It's not a lot, to be sure."

"Give me a number," Cameron said. "Something you feel might be close."

Susan gave him a number, and Cameron wrote it down. Then, one by one, he turned to each of the executive team members and asked the same question, carefully recording their answers.

The last was Stan Tetu. After he had answered, Cameron said, "One more question, Stan. What is your overall budget for marketing and advertising this year?" Stan thought for a moment, then gave Cameron a number.

"Let's see here," Cameron said, looking down as he did some quick calculations. He looked back up. "So based on this quick little survey, we spend about forty times more trying to bring in new customers than we do trying to retain our existing ones. That's four thousand percent."

He paused for a moment to let that sink in, then walked around the table until he was face-to-face with Humphries.

He looked at her. The CFO's face was hard and unflinching as she returned his steady gaze. "There's lots of evidence that we care about our customers' wallets," Cameron said to her softly. "But where is the evidence that we care about our customers?"

The room was silent as Cameron's message sank in. "He's right," Gerard said finally.

Syd looked at him and agreed. "Yes, it pretty much sums up everything I've been hearing over the last week." Gayle, with eyes still fixed on Cameron, slowly nodded in acceptance, as did everyone else in the room.

Cameron walked back to his chair and sat down. "One thing we're doing *right*," he said on a more positive note, "is that at least we're now starting to look at our organization from the right perspective—from the *customers'* point of view. We're asking ourselves the 'why' questions that our customers have been asking all along. We're getting glimpses of exactly how vulnerable we are. In this room, at least, we've lost the arrogance that we didn't even realize we had.

"As painful as this is," Cameron continued, "I'm really quite excited about where we are right now." He got a few skeptical looks at that comment. "Really," he insisted, "now that we're looking in the right places, we can start figuring out what needs to be fixed.

"And," he went on with the excitement creeping into his voice, "as long as we don't lose this focus, we'll make better decisions in the future."

"He's right again," Syd cut in. "For example, to be honest, I had no idea what was going on in our call center—and that's *my* baby." Cameron sat back down as the COO rose and leaned forward with both fists on the table.

"I championed the IVR system and the A.I. chatbots," Syd continued, "and I'm the one who decided that we didn't need a senior person looking after our customer service group—or external training to make sure they were doing a good job. I saw all that as expendable expense items on the financials—and eliminated them to keep us lean and mean." He looked down and smiled humorlessly. "But I hadn't counted on the 'mean' part quite so much.

"But before we run down there and start firing people," Syd looked back over to Gerard, "I think we have to take a look at where the issues really are. The truth is, your new friends Rachel and Daniel in the call center do what they do because they probably don't know any better. Who's coaching them? What's the skill level of the people leading them? Are we just running internal training developed by people with the same myopia that we seem to have had? I suspect that our customer service on the front line is just a reflection of the leadership around them."

"And the leadership around *them*," Gerard agreed. "It goes all the way up the line, doesn't it? Right here to this room. Right here to," he paused briefly, "me."

There was no response, as the people around the room studied the top of the boardroom table. It was Susan Tremmel who finally broke the silence. "I guess we're ultimately back to the original question," she said. "How do we fix it?" All eyes turned back on Cameron.

Cameron looked at each of them. "Truthfully," he said, "I have no clue. But I have a feeling that fixing it might end up being the easy part, once we've identified all the things that need to be fixed."

"You didn't talk with Daniel," Gerard grumbled to chuckles around the room.

"True," Cameron said with a grin, then said seriously, "but if we're all in agreement that customer experience begins with leadership, then we're on the right track. Look around this room. Is there any one of you not prepared now to make customer experience one of your priorities? We can't change the past. But we sure can learn from it."

Everyone nodded.

Syd looked at Gerard, then the rest of the room. "Cam's right again," he asserted, then with a sidelong glance at Cameron said, "I'm really getting tired of saying that.

"This is not a pleasant process," Syd continued. "I guess we shouldn't have expected it would be. So let's get back to it, shall we?"

And with that, he began sharing his experiences over the last week, beginning with his visit to Bartholomew's, a large chain of department stores owned by his close friend. He told them of the challenges their people in procurement faced, and how hard it was to reach live people.

"You'd think that, if our suppliers needed to talk with us, they could just call the sales rep assigned to their account," Syd said, turning to Tetu, "but apparently our sales reps aren't interested in talking with our customers unless they're placing an order. One of our biggest customers told me that they haven't seen one of our reps in their stores for two years! Apparently, they just sit around waiting for the telephone to ring."

Tetu reddened at this. "They get compensated on sales, not service," he said defensively. "We would have to change their whole remuneration structure."

"Ya think?" Syd growled. "Or maybe we can hire a few that value customers more than dollar signs."

"But it's even more than that," Syd continued. "Our competitors are kicking our butts in this. They have detailers out in the stores, facing shelves, making sure that inventory levels are sufficient, and that pricing is correct. They have product knowledge workshops, and incentive programs. They work with their customers during special promotions and events. We don't seem to have any of that." Cameron thought of the $10.99 Pressure Blenders at the Saggezza Center, and wondered when the last time a rep had been to that store.

"So, basically what I've seen in the last week from our customers' point of view," Syd continued, "is a company that sits around, waiting for the phone to ring, then won't answer it when it does. And just to make it a worse experience, when a customer actually *is* able to order something, we either don't have it in stock, we ship the wrong product, or we get it to them late.

"*Then*," he added, "to top everything off, we're just plain rude to them."

Syd's voice had gradually crept up in volume. He took a moment to compose himself, then continued, speaking softly and deliberately. "My old friend Sam Bartholomew told me that Household Solutions just wasn't worth their while dealing with. Honestly, if I was in his shoes, I wouldn't be dealing with us either." He sat down and looked at Cameron. "Don't get me wrong," he said seriously, "I do believe we can fix this. But it's going to be a lot of work for all of us." Nods again around the room.

The rest of the executives recounted their experiences in turn. Will Abbott explained how HR seemed far more interested in policies than they were in people, and made the point that internal customers were just as important as external customers. Stan Tetu detailed some punitive financial practices regarding late customer payments and payment of commissions to salespeople. Gayle Humphries identified how mistreatment of Household Solutions suppliers was impacting delivery times, and how logistics efficiencies always seemed to take precedence over customers' needs. Susan Tremmel echoed many of the things Gerard and Syd had noted, adding that marketing and finance weren't playing very well together.

Emotion flared as each executive found his or her department under attack. Cameron found himself several times having to intervene to move things along. Twice, Gerard had to stand and demand order. Two hours later, Cameron stood and looked around at an emotionally drained senior executive team.

"So, let me see if I've got everything," Cameron said as he tapped a few keys of the keyboard in front of him. He had been typing notes as people spoke, and they now appeared on the overhead LED screens. "Here are the 'why' questions we've uncovered so far. On the channel distribution side—our stores and wholesalers—we have: Why doesn't Household Solutions care about our business? Why can't we talk to someone when we need them? Why don't you get our orders right? Why don't you support your products better?" He continued to read all 16 items on the list. He then did the same for the consumer side, as well as for internal customers.

"I think this is a good start," Cameron said. "I know that many of these questions may not seem fair, but nevertheless they're out there." He quickly surveyed the room. Gerard looked to Cameron like he was almost beginning to smile. "The thing is," Cameron continued, recalling his conversation with Madeleine, "the way we perceive ourselves is irrelevant. If our customers think we suck, then we suck. Period. Fair has nothing to do with it. We have to keep collecting these questions, then find a way to do business so that customers don't feel compelled to ask them anymore."

He glanced at his watch. "I think we're done for the day. We'll reconvene next week and go at it again. Then, once everything is on the table, we'll put an action plan in place"

It was Stan Tetu's turn to speak up. "Just like that?" he asked. "From what we've discussed today, an action plan may take us months!"

Cameron nodded. "Perhaps. But, as I said, I really don't think it will. We're doing the hard part now—the digging and fact finding. The action plan is putting our creativity and experience together to deal with all of the issues we find. I suspect that's where we'll start having fun again. Albert Einstein had a famous quote: 'If I had an hour to solve a problem and my life depended on the solution, I would spend the first 55 minutes determining the proper question to ask, for once I know the proper question, I could solve the problem in less than five minutes.' I think the same will apply here. "

On that note, everyone dispersed. As he passed by, Gerard gave Cameron a pat on the shoulder. "Nice job, Einstein," he said. He was smiling.

CHAPTER
TWENTY-SIX

CAMERON MET MADELEINE THE next morning at the CappuGino's down the street from the Saggezza Center. Madeleine, with her usual flair, wore a vertically striped, fitted suit in lavender and white with a wide, 20s style collar, accessorized by a white fedora nestled on her platinum-blonde hair. She was relishing her Almond Toffee Latte, making soft ooing sounds with each sip. Cameron had ordered another Chiliccino, which he was finding quite addictive.

"So it sounds like you're making good progress!" Madeleine said encouragingly after Cameron had recounted the previous day's meeting.

Cameron nodded. "I think we are," he said. "But while we're doing a good job defining what's wrong, I'm not entirely sure I'll have a handle on how to fix it. I still don't have a clear picture of what 'Wow' customer experience looks like for Household Solutions."

Madeleine nodded as she set down her cup. "Well, let's do something about that, then. Shall we?"

They stood up, and Cameron said, "So today we'll be seeing Wow customer experiences?"

"I'll let you be the judge," Madeleine said with a smile, and began marching toward the Saggezza Center.

When they got there, Madeleine headed toward the elevators. "A new floor?" Cameron asked.

"Of course!" Madeleine said. "After all, you can't change what you see until you change where you stand." Cameron furrowed his brow and puzzled over that one.

The elevator doors opened, and Madeleine swiped her card and pushed the button for the second floor. Cameron again saw the button marked 'MOM' and was just about to ask about it when Madeleine let out an excited squeak. "OH!" she exclaimed, turning to Cameron. "I'd almost forgotten! Today is 'Towel Tuesday.' All of their bath towels are twenty-five percent off! The selection is fabulous too!" The doors opened, and they stepped out. "I'll meet you at the cash in forty minutes."

"It's going to take you forty minutes to pick out bath towels?" Cameron asked.

Madeleine gave him a scathing look. "Young man," she lectured, "one does NOT rush purchase decisions when it comes to bathroom decor."

Cameron tried his best not to grin, but obviously didn't succeed. Madeleine put her hands on her hips in mock disgust, let out a scornful "Hmph!" and flounced off into the store. Cameron watched her go, and gave up trying to hide his smile.

He knew the drill by now. He began with a quick survey of the store in front of him. Like the store on the first floor, the aisles were clean and wide, and the merchandise was well-stocked, well-organized, and accessible. Gone were the angry signs spouting rules and regulations. *So far, so good,* he thought.

All of a sudden, a voice came from his right. "'Nelpya?" it said. Cameron turned and saw a gray, unsmiling, young man staring at him.

Where do they find all these grey people? Cameron wondered.

"'Nelpya?" the man said again.

"Um," Cameron hesitated. "Thanks. I think I'm just looking for now."

The young sales associate almost looked relieved. "Okaywel

lI'llbeoverhereifyouneedme," he said and quickly walked away. Cameron watched him go, and gave his head a little shake.

What was that all about? he thought.

After a few more moments of reconnaissance, Cameron decided to head to the kitchenware section. *Might as well get the bad news over with early,* he thought. He began walking down the center aisle and saw another gray associate straightening up the shelves. *Well,* Cameron thought, *at least this floor has employees.*

He was a dozen feet away when the associate saw him. She hesitated for a few moments, then without changing expression said, "Nelpya?"

Cameron declined the offer, and the associate quickly turned back to the merchandise. Cameron walked past her, and was glancing back when another "Nelpya" came from in front of him. He turned and saw another gray associate who had appeared from around a corner. Again Cameron declined, and again the associate went about her business without breaking stride.

Good grief, Cameron thought. *This is probably supposed to be good customer service, but it sure doesn't feel right.*

By the time he reached the kitchenware section, Cam had been Nelpya'd seven times by seven gray associates. He watched as dozens of other customers got Nelpya'd too, and they didn't seem any more impressed than he was. The floor certainly appeared to have a lot more staff than the others he'd seen, but it didn't seem they were accomplishing much.

The kitchenware and small appliance section looked quite different in this store than the others. Plenty of display models were out, with little shelf-talkers highlighting the features of each product. There was ample inventory of everything, although it looked like they only kept in stock a few of the newer Household Solutions products. He was checking out the pricing when he heard another voice behind him.

"Good morning!" came a cheerful greeting. Cameron turned and saw yet another associate. Instead of the pale, gray pallor that seemed to typify employees around here, however, this young lady had healthy, pink cheeks and a decidedly perky demeanor.

Cameron matched her smile and said, "Good morning yourself!"

"How are you making out?" she asked, tilting her head a little, still smiling. "May I be of any assistance at all?" Cameron blinked. This was a pleasant change, he thought.

"Well," he began, trying to think of something to say. "I was looking for the Household Solutions Auto-Baste Broiler, but I can't seem to find it."

It was a three-year-old product, so he was pretty sure it wasn't going to be there.

The associate thought for a moment, then looked at Cameron apologetically. "Unfortunately, we don't carry that model anymore." Then back to her perky tone of voice, she added, "We do, however, carry these other two brands, which are very good." She directed his attention to similar products made by two of Household Solutions' largest competitors. Cameron sighed inwardly. He glanced at the associate's name badge. *Erin.*

"Erin," he asked, "why doesn't this store have the Household Solutions product? I've heard it's very good."

It better be, he thought. *I helped design it.* "You obviously carry other products from them. Why not this one?"

Erin nodded empathetically. "You're right. We carry most of the new products by Household Solutions. But this one's been around for a few years now, and I guess our buyers felt that these others would be a better fit for our customers."

Cameron nodded, trying to hide his frustration. Before he could think of another question to ask, Erin said, "I know you had the Auto-Baste Broiler in mind, but I do think you will be very pleased with either one of these other brands. They are very dependable, and if you decide you don't like it, we would be happy to take it back. We have a hassle-free return policy, and both of these companies are great with their warranties. Feature-wise, they're both pretty much the same. Is there one you think you'd prefer over the other?"

Cameron looked at Erin and smiled. Not only was her customer service good, she was a great salesperson, too. Quite a contrast to all the other, greay associates. "Are you sure you showed up for work in the right store?" Cameron asked.

A puzzled look came over Erin's face. "Excuse me?" she said.

Cameron gave a little wave. "Never mind," he replied with a smile. "I think I'll pass on the products for now—but Erin, thank you for your help—I really appreciate it."

"It was my pleasure," Erin said, the smile back on her face. "I hope we see you again!"

Cameron smiled back and said, "Me too."

CHAPTER
TWENTY-SEVEN

TWENTY MINUTES AND SEVERAL dozen Nelpya's later, Cameron had made his way to the front of the store. No sign of Madeleine. *How on Earth could it take so long to pick out bath towels?* Cameron found a good vantage point to stand and watch.

The first thing he noticed was the satisfying absence of the automated checkouts that were so prominent in the previous two stores. There were six cashes open, each with lines of three or four. Interestingly, while four of the cashiers were part of the uninspired gray retail army he had been seeing for the last couple of weeks, two of them were more like Erin. Bright, cheerful, talkative, they engaged each customer and truly looked like they enjoyed their jobs. Cameron had begun to think of them as Gray People and Real People.

It was a great study in social interaction. Cameron alternated his gaze from the slow, expressionless, gray cashiers to the others, and watched how very differently the customers responded to them. It was palpable. With the Gray People, customers looked serious, matter-of-fact, and unhappy. With the Real People, customers were smiling, talkative, and engaged. Even customers standing two or three back in line seemed happier.

Madeleine appeared at his side with her large shopping cart overflowing with towels. "Now THAT was fun!" she exclaimed. "Just look at those delicious shades!"

Cameron considered the multi-colored, terrycloth mountain. "You must take a lot of baths," he said finally.

Madeleine rolled her eyes and flipped her hand as if to say *whatever*. She adjusted a towel teetering at the top of the stack. "So I found what I was looking for," she said. "How did you make out?"

Cameron shifted his gaze back to the cashiers in front of them. "I certainly found something," he said, "but I'm not sure what." He described to her the Nelpya experiences and the great interaction he had with Erin.

He gestured to the cashiers. "Even here at the cash there appears to be some really good things happening—but it's just not all quite there." He turned to her. "I don't know if I'd call it great customer service, but it's a lot closer than the other two stores we've seen here."

Madeleine nodded in agreement. "Good," she said, and gave him an appraising look. "There's hope for you yet, young man," she smiled. "Now, let's pay for these things. There's someone else I think you should meet."

They directed the cart to one of the Real People. Even though there were two other people in line, she looked up and smiled at them. "Oh, HI Maddy!" she said excitedly, making eye contact with both of them. She turned and continued with the customer in front of her.

It took seven minutes for Madeleine and Cameron to reach the front of the line. *Interesting,* Cameron thought. Just the simple fact that he had been acknowledged by this cashier made the wait seem shorter. He watched her with the other customers. She kept up a pleasant banter while efficiently processing the purchases. He watched the customers' eyes as she worked. They were genuinely enjoying themselves. It was amazing, he thought, how much of a difference a smile and a few pleasant words made.

When it came their turn, the cashier's eyes lit up. "How ARE you, Maddy?" she exclaimed with genuine excitement. "Where have you BEEN?" Cameron saw her name tag—Lola.

Madeleine smiled back. "I know," she said to Lola. "It seems I just hardly have the time to shop these days!"

Lola nodded empathetically, and Cameron rolled his eyes. *Does this woman do anything else?*

Lola turned her smile to Cameron. "Hi," she said to him, "have we met before?"

Cameron thought for a moment, then shook his head. "No, I don't think so."

"Well, hi again then!" she said, extending her hand. "I'm Lola."

Cameron blinked and shook her hand, pretty certain that this had never happened at a store cash before. "Cameron," he replied.

"I'm pleased to meet you Cameron—especially if you're a friend of my favorite customer!" Lola said, putting the last of the towels into one of the eight large, plastic bags.

Madeleine waved her off. "Oh, pish! You say that to all your customers."

"Of course I do!" the cashier responded, then leaned forward and stage whispered, "but your my MOST favorite!" Madeleine smiled as Lola finished totaling up the bill.

She didn't even try to hand the bill to Madeleine. It was as if she knew better. With a sidelong glance at Madeleine, now preoccupied with lipstick and a small compact, Cameron handed Lola his credit card, and she completed the transaction. "Thank you, Cameron!" Lola said with her warm smile. "I hope we see you again real soon!" She then turned to the next customer. "Hi, Mr. Sedgwick!" he heard her say cheerfully.

"Wow," he said appreciatively as they walked away. "Now *that* is outstanding customer experience. Even I can see that!"

Madeleine stopped and looked at him incredulously. "Cameron!" she exclaimed disappointedly. "And here I thought we were making progress." She turned the cart and began wheeling it toward the office doors. "Lola is certainly wonderful—the best, if you ask me. But you hardly had an outstanding experience."

Cameron was confused. "I'm not sure I understand. One minute you're telling me that it wasn't an outstanding experience.

The next you're saying that Lola is the best. Make up your mind!"

He held the office door open as Madeleine pushed the cart through. "Cameron, we were *just* talking about it," she admonished. "How can we ever move forward if we keep having to repeat ourselves?" Cameron squinted. Yet again, he couldn't actually recall having such a conversation.

The reception area was a considerable improvement over the last two. The walls were freshly painted, and there was a colorful mural along one side. A single, new forest green divan sat in front of it. In an interesting anomaly, however, Cameron noted two tattered, gray couches bookended by two old, gray wooden chairs.

The receptionist was a short, slightly overweight young man with a friendly, lopsided smile. "Good morning," he said to them as they entered. "How may I help you?" A sudden look of recognition came to him. "Oh, hi, Maddy! How are you?"

Madeleine smiled back. "Hello, Walter. I'm doing wonderfully. More importantly, how are *you*? Do we have a big day yet?"

Walter's face brightened, and his smile grew wider. "This coming October," he said proudly. "I just asked her on Saturday, and she said yes."

"Well, congratulations!" Madeleine exclaimed excitedly. She waggled a finger at him. "Didn't I tell you that no woman could say no to a man like you?"

Walter laughed. "Aw, I don't know about that, Maddy. That amazing ring you helped me find played a big part, I think. Anyway, enough about me. How can I help you?"

"Is Ms. Miglio in?" Madeleine asked sweetly.

"She is," Walter said. "Is she expecting you?"

"No," Madeleine said. "But I'm *sure* she would want to see me."

"Who wouldn't?" Walter agreed, and reached down for the telephone. "But I'd better call to make sure—just in case." He tapped on a few buttons. "Ms. Miglio, Maddy is here and is wondering if you have some time for her." After a brief pause, he smiled and said, "Thank you, Ms. Miglio, I will tell her!"

He looked up at Maddy and Cameron. "Ms. Miglio would love to see you. Can you wait about five minutes? She said she wanted to finish something up so she can give you her undivided attention." Maddy thanked him, and they made their way to the green divan.

Cameron had been lost in thought throughout Madeleine's exchange with Walter. He sat on the divan in silence, staring at the floor. Madeleine just watched him.

"Consistency!" Cameron suddenly blurted out in a loud voice, causing Madeleine to jump.

"Excuse me?" Madeleine replied, straightening her hat, looking at him quizzically.

"That's why you said I wasn't seeing outstanding customer experience," Cameron said as much to himself as to Madeleine. "The cashier, Lola, was great, but our overall experience wasn't consistent. That was the conversation we had. While there were pockets of excellent service, it wasn't happening throughout the store. You're saying that it's not an outstanding customer experience if it's not consistent throughout an organization."

Madeleine just listened as Cameron continued. "But how is that possible? Based on that model and that definition, all it would take is one person's substandard performance to prevent an organization from becoming an outstanding customer experience provider. Nobody is that good. And if you take something the size of Household Solutions . . . well, we have thousands of people working for us around the world. That level of consistency just isn't possible."

Madeleine nodded sympathetically. "It's a daunting task, most definitely," she said. "But I think you're confusing perfection with excellence. I would agree that very few of us can be consistently perfect." She took a moment to smooth her skirt in a motion that suggested that this appraisal did not apply to her. "But I'm not at all convinced that excellence is unattainable."

Cameron thought about this for a moment. "But if we don't use perfection as our benchmark, then we end up with an arbitrary scale," he said. "If we accept imperfections, how do we define outstanding? How many imperfections or inconsistencies have to exist before we decide something is no longer outstanding?"

"Good question," Madeleine acknowledged with a smile. Cameron scowled at her. Madeleine appeared not to notice.

"Well, let me ask you a question," she said finally. "Are each of the products you manufacture at Household Solutions perfect?"

"Of course not—there's always a small percentage where something goes wrong." Cameron saw where she was headed with this, and nodded to himself slowly. "But we work to standards so the imperfections are the exceptions, not the norm."

Before Madeleine could answer, Walter's voice interrupted them from across the room. "Maddy, Cameron. Ms. Miglio will see you now."

"Wonderful," Madeleine said to Walter, then turned to Cameron. "Shall we?"

"We shall," he answered, standing and holding his arm out for her.

As they walked through the reception door into the inner offices, the first thing that struck Cameron was the openness of the layout. Gone were the maze-like hallways, replaced by a solid mass of workstation cubicles. It didn't look much different from the cube farms at Household Solutions.

Cameron noted with interest that about half of the cubes was that all-too familiar non-descript gray. They were interspersed with individual, brightly-colored cubicles, each decorated with equally colorful pictures and posters.

They walked past one area which Cameron recognized as their call center. A half dozen employees sat at their cubicles, wearing headsets and looking at monitors. He stopped for a moment and listened.

"Good morning!' the young woman closest to him said into the headset cheerfully. "Thank you for calling. How may I help you today?" She listened for a few moments, then said, "Absolutely, Ms. Feldon, let me take a look into this."

Cameron turned his attention to the next cubicle. It was one of the gray ones, with a decidedly gray employee inside. "G'morningthankyouforcallinghowcanIhelpyou," he said in a bored, monotone voice. Pause. And then, "Yergunnahafta talk to billing. Hold while I connect." *Amazing,* Cameron thought, *how completely different the experience can be depending on who someone spoke with.*

They slowly made their way counterclockwise around the

large open area, with the cubicles on their left and banks of offices around the perimeter. They finally arrived at the office in the far corner, with a small plaque reading R. G. Miglio. The door was open, and seated behind a functional, pine desk was a pleasant looking woman in her fifties with mid-length brown hair. She was plainly dressed—neither gray nor colorful. She looked up when she heard Madeleine's gentle knock on her door.

"Maddy!" she said warmly, rising to meet them. She and Madeleine exchanged double-cheek kisses, and Madeleine introduced Cameron.

"Rosa, I'd like you to meet Cameron Whitehall. Cameron is with Household Solutions and is on a quest to improve their customer experience. I know you've been working on it for some time now, and I thought you may be able to help."

Rosa shook Cameron's hand and gave him a warm smile. "We have indeed," she said, "although we're a long way from where we want to be."

"How so?" Cameron asked her, curious as to how she perceived her store's performance. They all sat, and Rosa explained. "When I got here five years ago, the customer service was horrible. The employees weren't friendly. They wouldn't even talk to customers beyond the bare minimum. Nobody really cared about the customers' experience."

Cameron nodded. *Just like the first two floors,* he thought.

"I brought in a training manager, and she brought in an outside company to train our staff," Rosa continued, "one that specialized in customer service. The difference was amazing. You could feel the change in energy on the sales floor. It didn't take with everyone, of course—I guess you can't expect anything to work one hundred percent. But overall, it made a real difference."

"That's good," Cameron said appreciatively. "Did you notice a difference in sales?"

"Absolutely," Rosa said, nodding emphatically. "Right away, in fact."

"Nice," Cameron said.

"It was very rewarding," Rosa agreed, then said seriously, "but, to be honest, there's still a big problem we can't seem to overcome." Cameron leaned forward with interest.

"The effect of the training only seems to stick with most people for a few months. After that, they fall back into their old habits again. Again, not with everyone, *thankfully*. Some people really got jazzed, and are able to keep their performance up. Unfortunately, though, that wasn't true with most."

Cameron thought about the Gray People and the Real People he had seen in the store. "How long ago did this training take place?" he asked.

Rosa glanced at the laptop in front of her and tapped on a few keys. "About two months ago," she said finally. "You see, we revisit our training on a regular basis for just this reason. Our training manager set up an internal university concept, which allows us to promote the continual improvement of our staff. We do more than just customer service training, of course, but with all of it, we have to retrain on a regular basis to keep people fresh."

"Is all this training worth it?" Cameron asked. "I mean, it sounds like a lot of time and money to have to keep training the same thing over and over again."

Rosa smiled at him. "You're absolutely right," she agreed. "It is both time consuming and expensive. But there's definitely a payoff. That's why we keep doing it."

"Having said that," she admitted, "it's still very frustrating. I'm sure there's a better way. I just don't know what it is. For now, we just have to keep driving the basic concepts home, hoping that a little bit more sticks each time we do it."

Cameron thought for a moment. On the surface, it certainly seemed they were making a diligent effort at improving their customer service. It supported Susan Tremmel's initial suggestions for a Household Solutions University. But, like Rosa, he couldn't help but think something was missing. He glanced over to Madeleine, who looked back at him with a smile.

"So what are you trying to accomplish at Household Solutions?" Rosa asked Cameron curiously. "I didn't even think that customer experience was on your company's radar screen."

"It wasn't," Cameron admitted. "We only just recently realized . . ." he paused, trying to think of a more diplomatic way to say "we sucked."

"That it was an area we needed to address," he said finally. "My job is to figure out the best way to improve things."

Rosa nodded. "You have a lot of work ahead of you," she said simply.

"So people keep telling me," Cameron said with a wry smile.

"Well, I've been there," Rosa said sympathetically. "Right at ground zero. And it's rewarding to see how much progress we've made. But we still have a long road ahead of us. I wish you well. Anything I can do to help, let me know. And if you figure out how we can more effectively get things to the next level, let me know that, too!"

"Most definitely," Cameron said. He looked over at Madeleine again, who was standing and reaching for her purse. A thought struck him, and he turned to look at Rosa. "Rosa, in your customer service training, what do you focus on?"

"Proactivity," Rosa responded simply. "We figure that if we can at least get our associates to start approaching customers, that's a good foundation. We've set up a ten-foot, ten-second rule in the store. Associates have to greet customers within ten feet or ten seconds. I have to say, they're getting quite consistent at it. What happens after that, though, is still pretty much a crapshoot."

Cameron thought about all the times he'd been Nelpya'd. "At least it's a start," he said to Rosa with a reassuring smile. He stood and shook her hand. "Thank you so much for your time. It was a pleasure to meet you!"

"Likewise," Rosa responded. She turned and smiled at Madeleine. "And you, Madeleine. Don't be a stranger!"

Madeleine smiled. "I won't. It's always such a pleasure to see you!"

They left her office and retraced their steps around the cube maze. Cameron looked at Madeleine expectedly. "Well?" he said.

Madeleine looked back at him quizzically. "Well what?" she asked.

"What is Rosa doing wrong? What's missing?" Cameron responded.

"How should I know?" Madeleine answered innocently. "I'm just a simple woman who enjoys shopping. All this talk about universities goes quite over my head."

Cameron grunted. "Give me a break," he said. "Seriously, it seems like she's doing a lot of the right things. What's missing?"

"Good question," Madeleine answered. Cameron just glared at her.

As always, Madeleine appeared not to notice. She stopped and held the door to the reception area for him. Cameron walked through, still glaring. "So," he said, his voice dripping with sarcasm, "if it's such a good question, why won't you answer it?"

It was Madeleine's turn to roll her eyes as she positioned herself behind her shopping cart and pushed it through the open door back into the store. "Okay," she said, talking with him as they walked. "I'll make you a deal. I will answer your question if you'll answer one of mine first."

Cameron grimaced. He was being set up again, and he knew it. "Deal," he sighed. "Ask away."

They stopped just in front of the cashiers. Madeleine turned to him with a sweet smile and eyes fluttering. "Cameron?" she began.

"Yes?" he said, bracing himself.

"What's the cure for cancer?"

Cameron blinked. "What?" he asked. "THAT's your question? How am I supposed to know the answer to that?"

Madeleine just looked at him. "It's a good question, though, isn't it?" she asked simply.

"Well, sure," Cameron said, frustration creeping into his voice. "It's a great question. The best. But it's not fair. How am *I* supposed to know the answer to it? I'm an engineer, not a scientist!"

"But it is a good question, though, isn't it?" Madeleine persisted.

"Yes. Absolutely. It's the best question ever," Cameron admitted, "but you're asking the wrong person!"

Madeleine had her compact out again and was peering in it. "Hmm."

Cameron stared at her for a moment. "You're suggesting that I should be talking to someone else," he said, nodding to her. "Okay, I get it. So who should I be asking?"

"Ooo," Madeleine's face brightened up and her eyes danced.

"Now that's an *excellent* question!"

"Maddy," Cameron said, "I have never had a migraine in my life up until today. Can we not play this game? Who do I need to talk to find out why Rosa's training programs aren't sticking?"

"Cameron!" Madeleine replied reproachfully. "For heaven's sake. That's a question you can answer yourself. Do I have to do everything around here?"

Cameron looked helplessly at Madeleine, then at the door to the office, then into the store. He turned back to Madeleine, put his finger up, then spun and strode purposefully into the store. Madeleine watched with interest and a hint of a smile on her face.

Half an aisle into the store, Cameron spied one of the gray associates and headed toward him. He was nine feet away when the associate looked up disinterestedly. "Nelpya?" he said.

"Actually, you can," Cameron responded. The associate looked dismayed.

"Can you tell me a little about your job?" he asked. "From a customer service point of view, that is?" A ripple of confusion came over the gray associate's face.

"Like," Cameron tried to think of a way to phrase it, "when you think of customer service in this store, what do you think of?"

"Tenfeettenseconds?" the associate said uncertainly.

"Yeah, I got that part," Cameron said to him dryly, "but what else? What else do associates do here to provide great customer service?

"Tenfeettenseconds." the associate said again. "Gotta greet the customer within ten feet or ten seconds."

"Why?" asked Cameron.

The gray associate wasn't quite sure what to make of Cameron. "I dunno. 'Cause it's important, I guess."

Oh dear heavens, Cameron thought inwardly. "Okay, let me ask a different question. I understand that you all do a lot of training here, is that right?"

At this, the associate nodded. "Sure," he said. "It's like a university."

"Right," Cameron continued. "So what else do they tell you that you're supposed to do when it comes to customer service?"

"Oh, they tell us lots of stuff," the associate said. "I don't really remember much of it, but it's usually pretty interesting."

"But you do remember the ten-feet, ten-seconds rule," Cameron said.

"Oh, yeah!" the associate replied. "Gotta know that one. Gotta do that one."

"Why that one?" Cameron asked.

The associate reached into his pocket and pulled out a piece of paper that began with "Congratulations!"

"When our supervisor catches us greeting a customer within tenfeettenseconds, we get one of these," the associate said. "It's worth five dollars in store merchandise."

"Nice," Cameron nodded.

"And if they catch us not doing it, we get in trouble." Cameron nodded again, the glimmer of understanding making its way into his brain. He thanked the associate, who seemed relieved to be released from all that customer interaction, and made his way back to a patiently waiting Madeleine.

"Well?" she asked expectantly.

"Well what?" he asked back innocently. *Two can play at this game,* he thought.

She narrowed her eyes at him. "Okay now THAT's just being childish! And HARDLY an appropriate way to thank me for all my help. I WAS going to offer to buy you one of Gino's new frozen Mocha-nillas, but perhaps I WON'T now!" She was just about in full flouncing-off mode when a now-grinning Cameron held up a hand.

"Okay, alright, you win!" he said with his arms spread dramatically. "But first I get the Mocha-nilla—*then* I talk."

Madeleine turned her head to look at him over her shoulder and considered. "Deal," she said after a moment of faux haughtiness, then resumed her flouncing out of the store. Cameron looked at her and grinned.

I guess there was no point in passing up on a perfectly good flounce, he thought.

CHAPTER
TWENTY-EIGHT

SEATED AT CAPPUGINO'S, CAMERON took a sip through the straw to his Mocha-nilla. He looked at Madeleine who was enjoying her Lychee-cran cocktail.

"So," Madeleine said, setting her glass down and looking directly at Cameron. "You have a theory as to why Rosa's customer service training programs aren't sticking?"

"I do." Cameron leaned forward, eyes looking upward as he searched for the best way to explain it. "There are three things, here, I think."

"Obviously, their greeting rule has stuck with everyone," he began, "and the other things they may have introduced in the training haven't. So clearly they're doing something different with that whole ten-feet, ten-seconds thing. The most obvious difference seems to be that there are tangible things attached to it. When they do it as they've been told, they're rewarded. When they don't, they get in trouble."

Madeleine nodded and smiled at Cameron. Her eyes sparkled.

"It looks like this is the only part of the training where they've created a direct, concrete link between the ideas presented in the training and the actual performance expectations on the sales floor," he continued. "The training is important, but the training alone won't necessarily translate into behavior in a live environment. They need something that reinforces the performance."

He paused for another sip of his Mocha-nilla. "It probably doesn't even have to be a tangible reinforcement. I'm guessing that it's mostly a management/leadership thing. When the managers and supervisors focus on something, so do the staff. People are focused on the ten-feet, ten-second rule ultimately because that's what Rosa is focused on."

Cameron looked at Madeleine to see if he was on the right track. "Keep going!" she encouraged him. "You're on a roll!"

"The second thing has to do with the *way* people execute the skills. I was curious as to why the Gray People all came up to me with 'Nelpya' or left me with 'Okay well I'll be over here if you need me,' but the Real People actually seemed to want to talk with me."

"'Gray People' and 'Real People'?" Madeleine asked with mild amusement. But it was pretty clear she knew what Cameron was talking about.

"I'm not sure what to make of it," Cameron confessed. "It's like there are some people in the stores who just have no interest in customers at all. They'd rather avoid us than talk to us. Why would someone take a job in customer service if they don't like dealing with customers?" he asked, not really expecting an answer.

"I'm thinking about what I've seen in the Saggezza Centre so far, and how it relates not just to Household Solutions, but to any organization. It seems to me that outstanding customer experience begins with having processes that make sense from the customer's point of view. If that's not in place, then you're sunk. It has to be easy for a customer to do business with us.

"Once that's in place, we have to make sure that our policies are focused on what's best for the customer, not what's best for us. We have to let people know that we're interested in them, and that they are important to us.

"This is the part where we move from being a profit-focused business to a customer-focused business to being a business that begins to earn real customer loyalty. That's where the people come in. You have to have people in place to look after customers. That's what begins to engage the customers.

"And it's not just having people use the right skills and say the right things," Cameron continued. "They have to actually be *interested* in the customers. They have to care. That's the difference between the Gray People and the Real People.

"The last element is leadership. They have to genuinely care, and genuinely believe that customers' experiences are the foundation of a company's success. Because if the leadership doesn't believe it, there's no way their teams will."

Cameron had begun speaking faster, as the concepts were rapidly crystalizing in his mind. "Some people just naturally care. Those are the Real People. They are the people who are probably self-motivated in everything they do in life, so it is just natural for them to be like that in their jobs. But the others— the Gray People—*need* the leadership. They need champions; a purpose; a rallying cry that gets them excited. Without purpose, it just becomes a job with a ten-feet-ten-seconds rule.

"All of this has to be consistent," he went on, "which means, for the people at least, there needs to be clear, meaningful, non-negotiable standards of behavior in place. There needs to be effective training so that people have the skills to execute them consistently. Then, leaders need to champion and inspect the performance regularly, and make sure that positive behavior is acknowledged, and substandard behavior isn't accepted."

Madeleine sat back with a proud smile on her face. "For a young man who just a few weeks ago didn't even know what shopping was, you've come a long way," she said.

Cameron smiled back, his burning eyes flickering downward with a slightly embarrassed look. "I should never have doubted you, Maddy," he said. "Now I just have to figure out how to translate all of this into something that will work for Household Solutions." He glanced at his watch. "And I guess I should get back there." He took one last sip of his Mocha-nilla, stood, and helped Madeleine with her chair. "So, what's next?" he asked.

Madeleine thought for a moment, adjusted her hat, and gave Cameron a look that seemed to ask if he really just said that.

Cameron grinned at her. "Same time, same place?"

"Marvelous idea!" Madeleine agreed, then winked, spun, and walked off just in time to miss the waitress showing up with the bill.

CHAPTER TWENTY-NINE

LATER THAT EVENING, AS Cameron sat in his living room, he felt a surge of excitement. He felt more pieces of his puzzle rapidly falling into place. "Okay, let's break this down into a logical sequence," he said to the bundle of fur flopped on the floor beside him.

Chewbacca cocked his head to one side and looked expectantly. *Food?*

Cameron grabbed a pen and opened his notebook on the coffee table. Leaning forward, he made notes as he talked it through aloud. "We begin with the end. How do we want Household Solutions to be perceived by our customers? We agreed that we want customers to think of us as delivering outstanding experiences from beginning to end. We're already there with our products, but what else do we have to address?" Chewbacca, realizing that food wasn't forthcoming, settled his head back into his paws, leaving one eye open to keep watch on his invisible tormenter in the corner.

"In order to really know this, we have to make sure we look at everything from our customers' viewpoint. Okay, we're doing that—at least we're trying as well as we can." He made a note to bring in an outside organization like the JMB Group to confirm what they were finding and give them a more objective, unbiased perspective.

"We need to look at our processes, to see where we have systemic issues that are getting in the way of the customers' experiences. We have to look for policies that, while well intended, either don't make sense to our customers or work against us being able to build relationships` with them. We have to have people in place who are engaged." He thought for a moment, and jotted down, *Real People, not Gray People*. He circled it to indicate this was one of the things he had to investigate. *How do we make sure we've got Real People?*

He looked down at Chewbacca. "Are you getting all this?" he asked. "There's going to be a quiz later."

Chewbacca's other eye opened and looked at Cameron briefly. *Bring it on.*

Cameron sat back on the couch and looked up at the ceiling. One of his biggest challenges, he knew, would be getting the executive team all on board. Since their last meeting, he had been tracking their progress. They were all trying, he knew, but he wasn't sure they really saw the big picture.

He thought about how his own attitudes toward customer experience had changed in the past few weeks. Before meeting his eccentric new shopaholic friend, he had always thought of customer experience as an add-on. Niceties. Something that was probably good to have, but still peripheral to the core of a business. He now understood that it was, in fact, the core of a business, and that everything else had to be built out around it.

Madeleine had helped Cameron view customer experience through the customers' eyes. Cameron had, in turn, tried to accomplish the same thing with the executive team. But he wasn't sure he had them quite where they needed to be. Right now they were still at the theoretical stage and focused on fact-finding and needs assessment. He looked at his notes. He was pretty confident they were at least on the right track. Was there still something he was missing? He thought about Madeleine, and wondered what she had in store for him next.

CHAPTER THIRTY

MONDAY MORNING CAME, AND Cameron was ready for anything the leadership team could throw at him. By the end of the meeting, he had vowed to himself, they were going to understand what it was like to be a Household Solutions customer. Worst-case scenario, he was going to personally take them to the Saggezza Centre.

To both his surprise and delight, however, every single one of the leadership team had independently come to the same conclusion without any further intervention from him. It began with, of all people, Stan Tetu.

"Cam," Stan began after the meeting had been called to order, "I have to tell you that your strategy of having us all dig into each other's business was brilliant." He looked over at Susan Tremmel. "It wasn't easy," he said with an embarrassed acknowledgement, "but truth be told, Susan's observations will transform our department."

"To be quite honest," Stan continued, "I learned far more than I ever expected to. Susan uncovered things that would frustrate any customer. Hell, if I was a customer having to deal with our company, I wouldn't buy from us either. It was embarrassing. There's no other word for it."

"Ditto with us," Will Abbot said, looking over at Stan. "And I'm pretty sure I owe Stan more than one apology for how ungracefully I dealt with *his* observations."

Stan nodded with an understanding smile and said, "No worries. Nothing you said to me comes close to what I said to Susan."

Will smiled back. "The fact is, though, you were bang on. And up until a week ago, I would never have connected the dots between the finance department and customer experience.

"There's a lot more, I suspect," he continued, "but now you've got me looking at my department in an entirely different light. I'm actually quite excited about making the changes. That is . . ." his eyes twinkled as he hooked a thumb toward Cameron. "Assuming our new boss lets me, of course."

And so it went around the table. Epiphanies, somber realizations, apologies, and relieved laughter. It was more than Cameron could ever have asked for. After everyone had shared their experiences, Gerard stood. He was smiling.

"I think I speak for everyone when I say, 'Job well done,' Cam," he said, looking over at his CCXO. "It would seem we have a long road ahead of us, but at least we now have an idea of where we need to go. So, I guess the big question is, what's next?"

Cameron was ready for this. "Thanks," he said to everyone as Gerard sat back down. "Thanks for all of the work you've done. I think it's fair to say that what we've done so far says a lot about this team.

"I don't really have the next steps completely figured out," he said, pulling a USB stick out of his top pocket, "but I have made some notes about the core elements of outstanding customer experience. I think this will help us stay focused and figure out where to direct our efforts." He stood, pressed a button, and the boardroom televisions began to glow. He inserted the USB stick into the console. "Let's begin by taking a look at the things we've identified," he began.

The word PROCESS appeared on the screen.

"We've found some ways to make it easier for people to do business with us," he said. "Stan highlighted this at the very beginning, but we're starting to see the surprising number of processes that impact our internal and external customers. It goes far beyond the IVR and our warranties. It includes the way we process returns, our shipping and receiving, our employee onboarding—just to name a few things.

"We found some policies that were focused on making our lives easier, but were irritations to our customers," he said as the word "Policies" appeared on the screen. "And some of our practices, such as salespeople who don't deal with customer experience issues, are costing us millions of dollars in direct business and customer loyalty." Now "Practices" flashed on the screen.

"These three areas, I think, are going to be the easiest fixes. The tough one is going to be our people. The thing is," Cameron said, "processes, policies, and practices are pretty easy to change once you've identified them. They are relatively finite—black and white. They are also easy to measure and track. People, though, aren't so easy." He thought about the Gray People and the Real People in the Saggezza Centre.

"It would be wonderful if we could just upload a Customer Service 2.0 app into everyone's brains, but people don't work like that." Cameron looked over at Susan Tremmel. "Even the university idea isn't enough, I don't think," he continued.

Susan nodded in agreement, then asked, "So what's the answer, then?"

"I don't know yet," Cameron answered truthfully, and his mind flashed to the eccentric Madeleine. "But I have a feeling I will fairly soon. In the meantime, what I suggest is that each of us go back to our departments, armed with the insights we've been able to glean over the last couple of weeks, and put together draft action plans to present next week."

Gayle Humphries nodded in approval. "I think it might also be a good idea to engage each of our teams in this process," she added. "Maybe offer an incentive for any ideas they can come up with that improves our service and experience levels."

Cameron quickly adjourned the meeting. *Always good to end on a high note,* he thought.

CHAPTER
THIRTY-ONE

THE NEXT MORNING, AS Cameron sat on a bench outside of the Saggezza Centre, he thought about how far he and the rest of the senior leadership team had come in such a short period of time. Change, he knew, was not easy, yet everyone seemed to be running with the shift to a customer-centric organization. He wondered why. True, no one had actually *done* anything yet, but there certainly didn't appear to be any resistance or passive bystanders in the group.

Perhaps, he thought, *it's because everyone first understood and accepted the why.*

That first day with Emily Seaborne—who clearly laid out the consequences of *not* taking action—was a big part of it, he knew. But there was more.

Leadership. The more he thought about it, the more he realized it all boiled down to Gerard Ogilvy's leadership. He still remembered that first meeting, after Emily Seaborne had left. The intensity of Gerard's demeanor. The unequivocal stand. "This is now everyone's top priority," he had said. There was no room for debate, and Gerard had wasted no time boldly appointing Cameron as Chief Customer Experience Officer. That unexpected and dramatic shift at the executive level, Cameron now understood, had been the clear signal that business as usual was no longer an option.

Leadership was also going to be the key to maintaining the momentum, Cameron knew. A desire for outstanding customer experience had to extend beyond the senior leadership team to every leader in the company. Then to every employee in the company. *But how do you do that? How do you take a passion that is shared by a few and transfer it throughout a company?*

He was so lost in thought, he hadn't even seen Madeleine come up beside him. Her now jet-black hair was tucked into a bright white flight attendant hat. She was wearing a black and white satin tuxedo pant suit with a small silk ornamental tulip on the left lapel. "Well, aren't you just looking serious today," she remarked, smiling as a startled Cameron looked up.

"If I've learned nothing else from you over the last couple of weeks," Cameron deadpanned, "it's that shopping is very serious business." He quickly appraised her outfit. "And that I clearly don't have enough clothes." He stood up from the bench and looked toward the big doors to the Saggezza Center. "So, I'm assuming you have plans for me today?"

"Of course!" Madeleine said. "But first, I'm *dying* to hear about yesterday's meeting! Are you making progress?"

Cameron told her as they walked together into the building and toward the elevator. When he was done, they had reached the elevator, and Madeleine was looking up at him, nodding with an approving smile. "Very nice, Cameron!" she said. "It's not easy to get people to accept change." Cameron thought he detected just a hint of sarcasm in her tone.

The elevator doors opened, and Madeleine pushed the button for the third floor. Cameron raised an eyebrow. "So I've graduated to the next level?" he asked.

"You have," Madeleine said, patting him on the shoulder.

CHAPTER
THIRTY-TWO

WHEN THE ELEVATOR DOORS slid apart, Cameron saw the difference instantly. The open, cheerful, brightly-lit store fairly begged him to enter. And it wasn't five seconds after he and Madeleine walked out of the elevator that they were greeted by an equally cheerful, tall, young man standing beside an enticing display of new spring merchandise.

"Good morning!" said the man, smiling effusively. Cameron thought he detected a Portuguese accent. "Thank you for coming in. Can I get you a cart, or a scanner perhaps?"

Alan, the name tag on his lapel read.

Before either Cameron or Madeleine could answer, though, Alan's eyes widened, and his smile broadened. "Miss Maddy!" he exclaimed. "How awesome to see you!"

Madeleine seemed just as excited to see him. "Alan!" she cried and spread her arms to give him a hug. "How is my favorite artist?" she asked earnestly, stepping back.

Alan shrugged his shoulders happily. "Up until ten seconds ago, I was great," he said. "Now, I am fantastic. How is the most beautiful lady in Los Angeles?"

"And," he turned to Cameron with a smile, "who is the lucky

man who has the pleasure of her company?"

Cameron smiled back. Madeleine turned to him and said in a loud stage whisper, "I know he says this to all of the girls he meets, but how can you not *love* it?" To Alan, she said, "Alan, this is Cameron Whitehall from Household Solutions. He is looking for insights on customer experience."

"Household Solutions ROCKS!" Alan exclaimed to Cameron unexpectedly. "That Single Serving Dishwasher has been a lifesaver for a simple store employee and part-time artist living in a bachelor apartment. You guys are brilliant!"

"Thanks," Cameron said. "That means a great deal to me to hear you say that."

"So you're doing some research into customer experience?" Alan said with interest. "I'm probably not the best guy to talk to about that. But you should totally talk to Mr. Vincente. If there is anyone who knows about customer experience, it's him."

Cameron thanked him and turned to Madeleine, who was pulling her phone out of her purse. "Is that who we're going to see?" he asked her.

Madeleine smiled. "If that's who Alan recommends, then that's the person to see," she said to Cameron as Alan beamed. "Although I think he's being a bit modest when it comes to customer experience, wouldn't you agree?" Cameron looked at Alan and nodded.

"First, though," Madeleine said with one finger in the air, "we do have some shopping to do. Is there anything I should know about, Alan?"

"Ladies spring fashion at thirty percent off." The young man gave her a knowing wink.

Madeleine's eyes grew comically, and she spun toward Cameron. "Did you HEAR that?" she said excitedly.

"I did," said Cameron with a resigned look. "I am trying to contain my excitement as we speak."

Madeleine's eyes narrowed to slits. "Are you mocking me?" she asked haughtily.

Cameron gave her an innocent look. "Mock *you*? Of course not. That would be rude. I just happen to be very good at containing excitement, that's all." He looked to Alan, but Alan was cheerfully greeting another customer. "I do have a question, though" he said, turning to Madeleine. "When Alan greeted us, he asked if we wanted a cart or a scanner. What was that about?"

Madeleine was not put off quite so easily. "Don't try and change the subject," she admonished. Cameron got the impression that she was enjoying being haughty. "You're just going to have to find out for yourself now."

"*I* am going shopping." She spun and flounced off toward the ladies wear section without looking back. It was the second time Cameron had witnessed this. He decided that Madeleine enjoyed flouncing at least as much as she enjoyed being haughty.

Cameron watched Madeleine leave, then turned his attention to the store. He watched Alan interacting with the customers. Not only did he seem to know a great many of them by name, but he was also able to remember an impressive amount of detail about each person.

Cameron realized that Alan was more than just an official greeter, as he had first suspected. He retrieved shopping carts for customers, guided them down aisles, and had animated discussions with them about every topic imaginable. When there were no customers to interact with, he cruised the aisles, making sure the merchandise was priced and in the right place. Every now and then he touched his ear and spoke into an unseen microphone. Moments later, an employee would appear and Cameron would watch Alan talk to him and gesture to an aisle or product. The two would inevitably share a smile or laugh before the employee headed off in the direction indicated by Alan.

Cameron began methodically walking through the store, and as he did, he saw several Alan-like employees. It looked like there were perhaps one or two in each department, all supported by a team of doers. They were in constant motion—fixing shelves, moving products, transporting merchandise from one place to the next. There weren't nearly as many as Cameron first thought, but they were in constant motion, and they didn't seem to be restricted to one area. They just showed up wherever and whenever they were needed.

Unlike other stores he'd seen, the people who worked there were far from just being task-oriented. It was clear that, despite their operational duties, customers were their number one priority. As with Alan and his colleagues, the doers stopped and helped, interacting and having conversations with the shoppers they encountered.

Cameron hadn't quite figured out the scanner thing yet, but he was quite intrigued by it. It looked like about a quarter of customers were walking around with small white devices the size of a television remote control in their hands. Every now and then, they would point it at an item, push a button, then walk away. Some would just glance at it. There were others doing similar things with their personal phones.

"Excuse me," he asked a young woman who was pointing her remote at a twenty-four pack of water bottles on an end aisle display and gazing at the screen. "Could you explain what that device does?"

"Sure," said the woman, looking over at him. "I only started using them a couple of weeks ago. They're awesome!" She walked over and stood next to Cameron and showed him the screen. "Anytime you see something you like, you just point at it like this," she said, pointed it at some jaunty, colorful umbrellas displayed beside the water bottles. "It reads that little code, then tells you about them."

Cameron looked at the screen and saw a picture of the umbrella, along with the product name, the price, the manufacturer, and a short description. Underneath was a button that said, *Related Products*, and another that said, *Customer Rating* and *Customer Reviews*.

"I can click on this," she pushed the *Related Products* button, "and I can see all the other umbrellas they sell." A list of products appeared on the screen as well as a selection of raincoats, boots, and hats. "And if I'm not sure which one to buy, I can click on this button, and read what people have to say about them," she said, clicking Customer Rating. Instantly, beside each product were a series of customer reviews, along with a rating from one to five stars.

"Then," the woman continued, "if I decide I want to buy it, I just push this green button that says Add to Cart, and voila! I'm done."

Cameron looked around and realized that the woman in fact, had no cart. "You mean, you don't put it in an actual cart?" he asked.

"Well, I *can*," the woman said, "but I find it much easier doing it this way." Seeing the confused look that had come over Cameron's face, she explained, "When I add it to my virtual cart, the store gathers up the items for me and has them bagged and waiting for me at the cash. I just have to check to make sure it's right, then I'm on my way."

"Just like that?" Cameron asked incredulously.

"Just like that. I can even just have it delivered if I don't want to lug everything home with me."

Cameron nodded thoughtfully, thanked the woman, and watched her walk away. His mind was racing. It was like the perfect blend of traditional retail and e-commerce. *Process*, he thought. *Could they have made it any easier to do business with them?* This was indeed impressive.

He suddenly thought about the people he'd seen in the store. He realized for the first time he had yet to see any Gray employees. All of the ones he had seen so far were totally engaged, pleasant, and seemed genuinely interested in the customers. He got the distinct impression that they really *cared*.

He began walking through the store, down one aisle and up another. He watched the customers, relaxed and happy as they walked through the store. Although everything seemed to be moving at a leisurely pace, there were a great many more—perhaps double—the customers than the other stores.

He wondered why it felt so much more pleasant. It felt cleaner, less claustrophobic, *friendlier*. As he looked around, he could see the subtle things that were contributing to the positive atmosphere. For starters, a lot of customers didn't have actual carts. That, combined with wider, less cluttered, better-lit aisles gave everyone a lot more space to move around.

Simple, friendly signs were everywhere, and there were interactive maps at the end of each aisle to help people find what they were looking for. *Practices*, Cameron thought. *It's amazing how much different a company looks when everything is focused on the customer.*

He turned a corner and found himself in the housewares and appliances section. As he stood there examining the displays, a thought occurred to him. He looked around for an employee, and found a middle-aged redheaded woman in an Alan-type role one aisle away.

"Excuse me," Cameron said. She turned and smiled brightly. Cameron saw the name Rebecca on her name badge. "Good morning!" she said cheerfully. "How can I help you?"

"Where can I get one of those nifty little scanners you use here?" Cameron asked.

"Just at the front of the store," Rebecca answered. "But if you have your phone with you, you can download our app and use it instead."

"Really?" Cameron asked.

"Absolutely!" Rebecca said brightly. "In fact, I can set it up for you right now if you would like." Cameron told her he thought that would be a great idea, and thirty seconds later he was looking down at the Saggezza Centre Shopping app on his phone.

"There it is," Rebecca said proudly. "Now all you have to do is fill out your information: name, address if you think you might like delivery, and so on. You can even put your credit card information in, if you would like to use the delivery service or our express checkout."

Cameron nodded and filled it all out while Rebecca stood by. When he was done, she said, "Let me make sure it is all set up right." She pulled out her own phone, peered at it, then back at Cameron. "Is it Cameron?" she asked.

Cameron blinked. "Er, uh . . . yes," he replied, not quite sure what just happened. Rebecca laughed. "I know—it's very cool, isn't it? The store's LPS tells me that you are standing right beside me. She showed him her screen, and saw a green dot with his name on in right in the center.

"LPS?" he asked.

"Local Positioning System," Rebecca answered. "It's like the GPS your car or phone has, but this is set up just in this store. That way, if you wanted to find, say, men's black socks," she took Cameron's phone, tapped a few keys and handed it back, "all you have to do is enter it, and follow the map." Cameron looked at his phone, and there was a map of the store with a green dot for him, a red dot labeled *black socks*, and a recommended route through the aisles.

Cameron looked up at Rebecca in amazement. "Thanks. This *is* cool!"

Rebecca flashed another smile at him. "My pleasure," she said. "Is there anything else I can help you with?"

Cameron shook his head. "Nope," he said. "Now I'm just going to play with my new toy."

As Rebecca walked away, Cameron turned back to the Household Solutions products. He saw a display of their new *Heat Surround Slow Cooker*, and four boxes. He pointed his phone at one of the boxes, pressed the View button, then looked at the screen. Sure enough, there was a picture of the product, the price, and a brief description. He tapped the Customer Reviews button. There were over fifty reviews. A brief scan revealed no surprises. Everyone loved the product, but there were more than a few warnings about the level of customer service and support provided by Household Solutions.

Cameron closed the app and slowly put his phone back in his pocket. *Time to find Madeleine,* he thought. He recognized the core of outstanding customer experience now, and he had some pretty good ideas how to translate what he had seen over the last few weeks into the manufacturing industry. *Policies, Practices, Processes* and *People*—with People playing the most important role. He just needed to learn how to create a customer-focused culture. That was leadership. Leadership was the last and most important piece of his puzzle.

He found Madeleine having an animated discussion with a young woman in the checkout area. The two were laughing and making wide gestures with their hands. "Speak of the devil!" Madeleine said when she saw Cameron. He gave her a concerned look, but was secretly happy that she was no longer flouncing.

"So," Madeleine said as she turned toward him, eyes twinkling. "What did you learn?"

Cameron smiled at her. "Well," he replied, "unless I'm mistaken, I think I've seen what outstanding customer experience is."

Madeleine beamed at him. "Well, *that's* exciting! So, what makes this so much different than the other places?" she asked.

"Well, for one thing, it all works together. Everything, the *People, Processes, Policies* and *Practices* are consistently customer-focused. I get the sense their people genuinely care about the customers in the store. And this scanning thing is genius. People get the tactile experience of shopping with the convenience of e-commerce."

"Oh, you learned how to use the scanner!" Madeleine said, impressed.

"Well, I got the app on my phone," Cameron replied, and pulled out his phone to show her. "It's very cool."

Madeleine took it and looked at it appreciatively. "These *are* a nice touch," she admitted, as she tapped on the screen. "So much nicer than having to carry things around with us. Not only did I save almost two hundred dollars today, but I have a whole spring wardrobe being delivered to my house at 7:30 tonight!"

Cameron nodded as she handed his phone back. "All I have to do is figure out how to apply these principles to Household Solutions," he said, "which I think we can do.

"The big issue, I think," he continued, "is understanding the leadership side of things. How have they managed to get everyone on the same page?"

"EXCELLENT question!" Maddy said excitedly. "Let's go and talk with someone about that, shall we?" Cameron nodded, and the two of them began walking past the cashier. Alison, Cameron saw, was on her name badge.

"It was *great* seeing you again, Maddy!" Alison said with a big smile. Then, turning to Cameron, "And thank you, Mr. Whitehall, for shopping with us!"

Cameron smiled back. "Well," he confessed, "I didn't actually shop, but I did have a great time." Alison and Madeleine exchanged glances, and both giggled softly. Cameron groaned as he remembered Madeleine taking his cell phone. Apparently he had gone shopping after all.

CHAPTER
THIRTY-THREE

MADELEINE LED CAMERON TO a large, modern s-shaped desk in the main foyer behind the cash area. Cameron had noticed it before, and had assumed it was a customer service desk. But he realized now that it was actually a reception desk of sorts. Reception to where, however, he couldn't tell. There was no obvious office entrance.

As they walked up, one of the three receptionists broke into a smile and said, "Good afternoon, Maddy! Good afternoon, Mr. Whitehall! You are here to see Mr. Vincente?" Cameron was confused momentarily. *How on earth did she know who we were?* he wondered. Then he remembered the app on his cell phone. But how did she know who they were going to see? The answer made its way into his head a second later. *Alan,* he thought. *Alan must have let Mr. Vincente know we were coming.*

"Is he available?" Madeleine asked sweetly. "Of course!" came the reply, in a tone that suggested Madeleine should know perfectly well he was always available to her. "Do you know where his office is?"

"Of course!" Madeleine said, echoing the receptionist's tone. They both laughed. "At the end of the hardware department, at aisle fifty-seven," Madeleine said knowingly. The receptionist and

Madeleine waved to each other, then Madeleine took Cameron's arm.

Madeleine led Cameron counter-clockwise along the perimeter of the store. As they walked, Cameron noticed for the first time that the outside walls of the store were really offices with glass walls and glass doors. There were hundreds of them, he thought. He stopped suddenly and looked behind him. Madeleine stopped with him.

"Isn't that Alan?" Cameron asked, pointing to an office they just passed. Madeleine looked. Sure enough, there was Alan sitting at a desk having an animated conversation on the telephone.

"I believe it is," she replied.

Cameron looked at the name on the door. *Alan Muirhead. Vice President of Marketing.* "He's the VP of Marketing? The VP of Marketing greets customers in the store?" he said incredulously.

"So it would seem," Madeleine said, not appearing the least bit surprised. Cameron looked at her, but she didn't expand. As they continued walking, Cameron began to read the names and titles on the doors of the offices they passed. *Director of Talent Development, Senior Buyer.* Looking into the offices, Cameron recognized at least three more faces he had seen out on the sales floor—people he originally thought were simply store supervisors. *Did they all work in the store,* he wondered?

They reached the hardware department and, across from it, the door that said *Avi Vincente, CEO.* Through the glass Cameron saw a middle-aged man, who he assumed was Avi Vincente in a patterned white dress shirt and silver pants talking casually with a young, dark-haired man who appeared to be in his early twenties. Even from a distance, Cameron was struck by the CEO's eyes. They were like rich golden prisms that captured the ambient light and beamed it at whatever they focused on. The contrast to the white irises and his short, curly, midnight-black hair was compelling.

As they approached the door, Vincente turned, smiled and waved at Madeleine and Cameron. Madeleine smiled back and gave him a little finger wave. The CEO gestured for them to come in.

"Madeleine!" he exclaimed when they entered, turning and stepping forward to give her a warm hug. "I am so happy to see you!"

"And I you," Madeleine replied with a wide smile followed by a feigned serious look. "But Avi," she admonished sternly, "a man in your position really *shouldn't* display such public affection. People will start to *talk*."

Vincente let out a delighted bark of laughter. "Let them!" he proclaimed loudly with a theatrical spread of his arms. "To be seen with a lady like you does nothing but enhance my reputation!" Cameron couldn't be sure, but he thought he actually saw a slight blush on Madeleine's cheek.

Vincente shifted his gaze to Cameron, and with a glance back at Madeleine, he asked her with mock concern, "But it appears there is another man in your life. Should I be concerned?" He extended his hand to Cameron. "Avi Vincente, at your service," he said in a rich, genuine baritone. Their eyes locked momentarily, and in that brief moment Cameron knew this man was the person responsible for the company's success.

Cameron couldn't help but smile back. He found himself immediately liking and trusting this man who seemed to project confidence, competence, compassion, and passion all at the same time. The only other person he had ever met with these qualities was his own CEO, Gerard Ogilvy. He grinned at Vincente as he shook his hand. "I have a feeling that the lady has many men in her life. Cameron Whitehall. Pleased to meet you."

"The pleasure is absolutely mine," Vincente said earnestly, then gestured to the young man standing next to him. "Please let me introduce my colleague, Fabiano Ferreli. He moved here from Brazil a few years ago and is a wonderful new addition to our company."

Cameron and Madeleine took turns shaking Fabiano's hand. When the introductions were done, the young man reached for the door to make his exit, but stopped when he felt his CEO's gentle hand on his shoulder. "Please," Vincente said to him softly, "stay. There is much you can learn from this beautiful lady." Fabiano tried to suppress a doubtful expression as he glanced over at the older woman.

"Umm . . . I would love that," he said almost convincingly.

Vincente grinned even wider. "Excellent!" he proclaimed, then turned so that he was facing Madeleine. He looked at her for a moment, and his grin transformed into a concerned look. "So, have you come to check up on me?" he asked. "To see if I actually learned anything from you?" He pointed at his ears. "I know it doesn't always seem that way, but I really do listen, you know."

Madeleine smiled and waved her hand dismissively, digging around in her purse for her compact. "Oh, pish. What could an important man like you possibly learn from a simple woman like me?"

Vincente and Cameron both looked at each other with amused expressions. A second thought suddenly hit Cameron. Vincente, he realized, had been through a similar journey with Madeleine. He and Cameron were kindred spirits.

"Only *everything*," Vincente replied in answer to Madeleine's question, bowing slightly to her. Madeleine ignored him.

Vincente shrugged his shoulders. "Cameron," he said in a resigned tone, motioning everyone to sit. "I suspect I am more likely to get straight answers from you. Please tell me. How may I be of service?"

Cameron sat down and leaned toward Vincente. He was eager to hear what this man had to say. He told Vincente about his mission with Household Solutions, the steps he had taken so far, and what some of his thoughts were. Vincente leaned back in his chair, fingers tented under his chin. His eyes burned with intensity.

"To be honest, Mr. Vincente," Cameron said, "the things that seem to be happening in this store are exactly what we need to have happening in our company. I guess I'd love to know how you did it. Everything here seems to be running so smoothly. And all of your people seem so . . . engaged. They seem one hundred percent customer-focused. If you can provide me with any insight, I would be forever grateful."

Vincente nodded slowly, then spoke. "Please," he began, "call me Avi." He spread his hands wide in front of him. "I'll be delighted to help as much as I can. I'm very proud of how far we've come, and we couldn't have done it without a lot of guidance." He glanced over at Madeleine with a smile. She appeared not to notice. He looked at Cameron "It's nice to have an opportunity to pay it forward, so to speak."

Cameron nodded. He hoped he would be in the same position someday.

Vincente stood and gestured to the store outside of his window. "Perhaps the most important thing I've learned," he said, "is that there is no end to the journey of creating an outstanding customer experience environment. A day doesn't go by that I don't meet someone with ideas on how we can improve.

"Take my new colleague, Fabiano, for example," he tilted his head to the young man standing in the room. "Since finishing college two years ago, he has been working in security at the container port down in San Pedro. If you had asked me yesterday what role customer experience might possibly play in an environment dedicated to moving great big shipping containers from one place to another, I would have struggled for an answer. But now I understand how critical it is—even for the people working in security roles.

"The thing is," Avi said in earnest, "customer experience is a moving target, with customers' expectations changing and increasing every day. What was good enough to stand out five years ago is not good enough to stand out this year. What was good enough to stand out one month ago might not even be good enough to stand out this month. One must never get complacent.

"In fact," he continued as Cameron nodded, "I would argue that it is the very moment at which one believes they have mastered customer experience that they begin the slide to mediocrity. There are too many other companies competing for the same customer. They are pushing the bar every day. If we stop to pat ourselves on the back for too long, they will quickly surpass us."

He paused for a moment and regarded Cameron. "There are, as you undoubtedly know by now, many difference facets to customer experience. Is there any specific area in which you are looking to focus on?"

Cameron chuckled at this. "The short answer is—*everything*," he said. "But I'm guessing you won't have time for that."

Vincente smiled at him. "I will make time," he said simply.

"Where do you foresee the biggest challenges in making Household Solutions an outstanding customer experience company?"

Cameron already had the answer for this one. "I have a lot of confidence in our executive team to do some wonderful things with our operations—our policies, processes, and practices. It's the people side of things I'm not sure I understand."

"Out here," he waved an open hand to the bustling store on the other side of the window, "you appear to have your people delivering a consistent, great experience. I have yet to see an exception. How did you accomplish this?"

Vincente bowed his head briefly, then looked up with a knowing smile. "Ah," he said with a touch of pride in his voice, "you speak of my garden."

CHAPTER
THIRTY-FOUR

BEFORE CAMERON COULD ASK, Vincente continued. "Forgive my indulgence," he said modestly. "I was raised in a small village in central Italy—in the Tuscany region just south of Florence. My parents had a small vineyard, and a humble but successful vegetable farm."

"When I turned eight, my father took me out into the fields where he had cleared a small area—about twenty feet by twenty feet. He told me that this was mine. I could plant anything I wanted, and when harvest time came, I could sell what I had grown at the local market.

"I was very excited, and took to the task with the enthusiasm reserved only for the very young. What I didn't realize until many years later is that my father wasn't just teaching me about gardening—he was teaching me about life and leadership."

"I learned five lessons from my garden that I have taken with me wherever I have gone. They have helped me grow strong teams that have led to successful businesses."

Avi leaned back in his chair and looked up at the ceiling, as if recalling a distant memory. "The first lesson I learned came at my first harvest. I had planted a great deal of corn in my garden that spring, because I had always loved how majestic and tall it grew. I recall becoming more and more excited as the summer drew on, and so proud watching the corn stalks—*my* corn stalks—reach for the sky. By August, I harvested almost two hundred ears of corn. I knew how much I could sell each ear for in the market, and how much in total I would earn. It was a great deal of money for an eight-year-old boy!

"My father watched me loading my corn onto the cart to take to the market. He was smiling. Before we left, he asked me how much money I was expecting to make. When I told him, he nodded, still smiling, then broke the news to me. It turned out that the type of corn I had planted was feed corn instead of the sweet corn intended for people. He explained that there were farmers who would no doubt buy it from me, but that I would be getting only a fraction of the amount I was expecting.

"I was devastated, but I never forgot the lesson: *Plant the right seed.* It was my first lesson in goal-setting—that you can't expect to harvest something when you haven't first planted the right seed. All too often, people in leadership positions expect certain outcomes, or for people to behave in certain ways—but they haven't first planted the seed for it. They don't make any significant effort to either communicate their expectations, or clear the path to facilitate a positive outcome."

The truly sad part is that, rather than recognize their own mistakes, most of these leaders just blame their team for the disappointing outcomes." Avi gently shook his head. "It's ridiculous that we do this, of course. It would be like me blaming the corn plant for not producing the right kind of corn. But one sees this far too often."

Cameron had been listening intently. "I've seen this very thing, *and* the impact it can have on the team," he said. "Although I've never thought of it quite in these terms before."

"It seems to me," he added, "that *plant the right seed* is also a lesson for making sure you hire the right people for the right roles in the first place."

Avi nodded enthusiastically. "Absolutely!" he said appreciatively, making a point to look at Fabiano. "That's where it all begins."

He leaned forward and looked at Cameron. "The second lesson from my garden was: *Help things grow.* Things grow better when you help them. Plants, like people, *want* to grow. They want to become taller and stronger. They want to blossom. Some can do this on their own, some cannot. The greatest success and the greatest consistency is achieved when someone is there to ensure they are getting sufficient nourishment and conditions are in place for their success. You water your garden each day—sometimes twice—add nutrients to the soil, and so on.

"Too often we expect our teams to grow and flourish, but we don't provide them with the conditions they need to succeed—things such as good working conditions, adequate training, or a meaningful support system."

Cameron had pulled out a notepad and was writing furiously. He looked up at Avi. "The analogy is amazing," he said, "and I agree completely. But I'm not sure how this relates to influencing your customer experience."

Avi nodded and smiled. "Fair point," he replied. "It does at first seem somewhat peripheral to the topic of customer experience. But it is, in fact, quite critical. It is most certainly essential when it comes to customer *service.*"

Avi gestured toward Madeleine, who had been sitting with a slight smile, quietly observing the interaction between the two men. He continued. "As the beautiful lady beside you has no doubt shared, customer service is not simply common sense, as most would have you believe." Cameron nodded. He remembered the conversation.

"To create the level of performance you are looking for," Avi went on, "one plants the right seeds at the beginning—and you do this by sharing with everyone what the vision and expectations are. But that alone is not enough. You must help your team grow. You need to help them understand and master the skills to execute your vision consistently. They need to have the physical and intellectual tools to continually improve.

"Many of the customer service skills people need may seem straightforward, simple, or common sense, and most everyone believes that they are already pretty good at them. But all you have to do is compare the performance of a real superstar to that of the average person, and you realize how much room there is for people to grow." Cameron nodded again. He had seen this first-hand as well.

"We do a lot of ongoing training in customer service," Avi continued, "and it makes a big difference. We bring in people who are experts. People who can help us look at seemingly ordinary things in extraordinary ways. We teach our internal leaders how to champion customer service and help people refine their skills in the live environments."

Cameron grimaced briefly as he glanced at his hastily written notes. He wondered if he was actually going to be able to read them later on. He turned to Madeleine, who seemed to be gauging Cameron's reaction to Avi's insights.

"Why didn't you introduce me to Avi when we first started this?" Cameron chided her.

Madeleine just gave Cameron a shrug and continued to smile. Avi continued as though he hadn't heard.

"The third lesson I learned was how important it is to *always track progress,*" he said. "In the second year of my garden, I had planted six varieties of lettuce. There was good rain that year, and everything seemed to be growing so well that I stopped checking on it."

"One day, at suppertime, my father casually asked me how my lettuce was doing. I told him that, with all the rain, we should have a record crop. He paused for a moment, then suggested we go outside for a walk. I knew at that moment something was wrong."

"Sure enough, when we got to my lettuce patch, I saw that much of it had been eaten, or partially eaten, by animals. My father told me that a family of rabbits had started showing up a week ago. They had also helped themselves to the beets he had been growing. The difference, though, was that my father had noticed what they were doing after the first day, and had surrounded his beets with a small chicken-wire fence, just tall enough so the rabbits couldn't get in.

"By the end of that evening, I too had a fence around my crop, and I managed to save about half of it. But it was a painful lesson in the importance of awareness and vigilance is. It's absolutely true that 'you can expect what you inspect.' Since that day, I have always been aware of what is happening in my garden.

"It has proven an invaluable lesson when it comes to the customer experience performance of our team," Avi continued, his arm sweeping in a large arc to indicate the store. "How can we create consistency if we, the leaders, are not aware of what's going on? How can we help our team raise the bar if we don't know where the current bar is?"

"I understand what you're saying," Cameron interjected with some uncertainty, "but inspecting all the time . . . isn't that kind of . . . well . . . micromanaging?"

"Some may feel so," Avi acknowledged, "and it is a delicate balance between being on top of things and being in the middle of things." He looked at Cameron, who again sensed the power in the CEO's rich, golden eyes. "But is it really any different than the quality control practices you use in your manufacturing?"

Cameron thought about this for a moment, then nodded slowly. "No," Cameron said. "No, it is no different at all." He began to scribble in his notebook.

Avi waited for Cameron to finish his notes, then held up four fingers. "The fourth lesson, *Don't allow weeds to grow*, came the very next year. I planted carrots that year, and, coincidentally, my father had allocated a similar space for his carrot crop."

Avi smiled wryly as memories entered his consciousness. "I used to think my father was unduly obsessive about weeds," he said. "It seemed he was always fussing. He refused to use chemicals, so he was constantly walking the crops, extracting any weed that had the audacity to try to make a home there.

"By this time, I was eleven years old with a lot of friends and a lot of interests. I certainly didn't have time to be worried about a few weeds. So, for the most part, I didn't bother too much with them. Every now and then I would haphazardly remove a few of the really big ones which had gotten out of control, but that was it."

"When it came time to harvest, I was shocked to see that, not only did my father have a great many more carrots from his crop, but they were much, much larger. I didn't understand, and actually became angry, thinking that perhaps my father had just used some special fertilizer.

"When I confronted him, he simply pointed at my garden, full of weeds, and said, 'What did you expect? You allowed all of those weeds to take up valuable space and suck the nourishment out of the soil. How could you possible expect your crop to grow under those conditions?'"

Avi laughed softly as he continued. "And he didn't stop there. He had had enough of this irresponsible child. He took my hand, walked me to the edge of my garden, and pointed at it in disgust. 'Not only did you hurt this year's crop,' he said, 'but if you don't do something, you may not have a crop next year at all!'"

"When I asked him what he meant, he pointed again to all of the weeds, then explained to me that, because I had let them grow so long, they had now dropped their own seeds in my garden. Which meant that there were going to be fifty-fold as many weeds next year.

"He was right, as usual, and the next year began with my garden being virtually choked with every manner of weed. Determined not to let them beat me, I dedicated the whole spring to removing them—and catching all of the little ones before they had a chance to get a foothold. Needless to say, my crop improved dramatically, and my workload was considerably less in the following years.

"In business, weeds are the attitudes and behaviors of the people we have working for us," Avi said. "When they are negative, they will suck the nutrients out of a workplace—just as weeds do in a garden. You can't let them take root. You have to address them immediately.

"Sometimes," he said sadly, "you can find yourself unable to convince someone to change to a more positive and productive mindset. And most times, in most companies, we just let these people be—and try to either rationalize or ignore their behavior. But, just like weeds in a garden, if not removed, that person's presence will have implications throughout the organization."

Cameron had stopped writing and was looking intently at Avi. "So, you're in or you're out? Is that what I'm hearing?" he asked. He was surprised that this charismatic individual would espouse this seemingly heavy-handed approach.

"When it comes to how well we treat each other and our

customers," Avi responded without hesitation, "absolutely." He seemed surprised that Cameron would have asked that question. "What do you do when you find a substandard part in one of your products?"

Cameron closed his eyes and winced at the obviousness of Avi's point. "We would remove it instantly, of course," he said, looking directly at Avi, who had allowed himself a little grin. Cameron looked over at Madeleine, who had assumed a somewhat bemused expression herself. "It appears you aren't the only one who enjoys it when I say stupid things," he said to her. Avi laughed out loud.

"Believe me," he said with a sidelong glance at Madeleine, "I understand exactly how you feel!" Cameron had no doubt that he did.

"The final lesson I learned from my garden was: *Provide sunshine,*" Avi went on. "Nothing grows without sunshine. Plants need abundant sunlight. They need the warmth and energy to grow and thrive." He gestured upward. "For a garden, of course, the sunlight comes from above. The same is true in our businesses. Our people need our energy, our inspiration, our motivation."

"These are particularly important when driving a customer service culture. If we aren't passionate—visibly and demonstrably passionate—we will never be able to instill this in our people. We can never lose sight of the role we play in the success of our organization."

Avi had become quite passionate as he continued to speak. He paused for a moment, leaned back in his chair, and looked apologetically to the people in the room. "Gracious," he said, "I seem to have delivered quite the lecture! It is not really my nature to go on so."

"Are you kidding me?" Cameron said, leaning forward with an excited expression, "I can't begin to thank you enough." He had also figured out why Madeleine hadn't introduced him to Avi earlier. Without the experiences over the last few weeks, most of the CEO's insights would have been lost on him.

"You've got my brain going a hundred miles an hour," Cameron continued with obvious excitement in his voice. "I'm already starting to get flashes of how this all fits into our picture at Household Solutions." He leaned back with a satisfied look on his face. "All I have to do is translate these principles to our environment, and we are on the path to creating the customer-focused culture and the 'wow' experiences we're looking for."

Avi and Madeleine exchanged glances. Cameron eyed them suspiciously. "What?" he asked, looking from one to the other. "Don't tell me I'm still missing something."

Avi raised his eyebrows and looked at Madeleine. "He hasn't seen it yet?" he asked with surprise. Madeleine smiled sweetly. "We had shopping to do," she said matter-of-factly, as though this explained everything.

She rose, and Cameron, Avi and Fabiano, taking her cue, followed. She gave Avi a brief, warm hug, then stood back and said, "I am very proud of you, you know." Avi said nothing, but Cameron was surprised to see a hint of redness rising through the confident CEO's cheeks. Handshakes all around, Cameron and Madeleine turned to leave the office.

"Cameron," Avi said. Cameron turned.

"I would very much like to hear how your journey goes," Avi continued. "Please keep in touch. And if there are any other insights I might provide, just come by my office. My door is always open to you."

Cameron smiled and promised that he would. Then, realizing Madeleine had already marched on ahead, he spun and sprinted after her.

CHAPTER
THIRTY-FIVE

CAMERON WALKED IN SILENCE as he followed a half-step behind Madeleine toward the front of the store. He was thinking about Avi's five leadership lessons. So simple, so obvious, yet how many organizations really embraced them? And he knew that these five principles would have to be in place at Household Solutions before any attempts to create a truly outstanding culture would stick.

He thought of Alan and all the other leaders—so in tune and in touch with their customers, and the seamless communication throughout the organization. What would that look like at Household Solutions? He was also very curious about this last piece of the customer experience puzzle Maddy had not yet shared with him. It was hard to imagine there was a level beyond what he had already seen.

The elevator doors opened soundlessly as they approached, almost as if it knew they were coming. Once inside, Madeleine pushed the button labeled "MOM." *Ah,* Cameron thought to himself, *I'm finally going to see what this is all about.*

"So, Cameron," Madeleine began, breaking the silence. "You are very quiet."

Cameron looked at her. He realized how lost in thought he had been. "Sorry," he said. "I'm just trying to process all of this."

Madeleine nodded with a knowing smile. "Indeed," she said. "Do you think you're ready for a little more?"

"Bring it on," Cameron said, although somewhat unconvincingly. "I'm ready."

The elevator doors opened, and Cameron followed Madeleine out into what appeared to be an elegant reception area. The walls and decor were pure white, accented with hints of browns and beiges. On the textured white floor tiles lay a massive, rich, thick carpet that looked more like a piece of art than something people should walk on.

The reception desk was actually three white oval workstations—each featuring soft, leather chairs and a pleasant looking employee.

The only workstation without a customer was the one in the center. The young employee stationed there saw Madeleine and Cameron and stood up instantly. "Good afternoon," he said with a smile as he came around the desk and extended his hand. "You must be Maddy and Mr. Whitehall. "

"We are indeed," Cameron acknowledged, taking the young man's hand, "and you must be psychic."

The greeter laughed. "I *wish*," he said. "It sure would make my job a whole lot easier! My name is Gary." He gestured to the two chairs. "Please, have a seat."

"So," Gary said once they were settled, "how may I help you?"

Madeleine introduced Cameron and said, "I was hoping you might be able to tell Cameron a little bit about what you do here."

Gary beamed. "Of course! Our goal here is to make sure that we are doing everything within our power to create the best possible experience for our customers."

Cameron was intrigued. He thought that's what was happening on the floor they just visited. "And how do you do that?" he asked.

Gary paused for a moment, considering the best way to answer Cameron's question. "Well," he said, "here we look for opportunities to really connect with our customers on a very personal level."

"You see," he said, "most companies like ours—ones that have a lot of customers—rely heavily on their processes and larger-scale initiatives. They take advantage of economies of scale and efficiencies to maximize their profit levels."

Cameron nodded. He understood. Gary continued. "We do that, too. But we also understand that, while these processes and initiatives are important, they aren't the things that create *customer loyalty*. And loyalty from customers is, ultimately, what sustains a business."

Cameron nodded again. This was the tough lesson Household Solutions was learning, he thought. Gary gestured to the three of them seated around the desk. "Loyalty is a two-way street," he said. "It's basic human nature. We are loyal to people who are loyal to us. We look after the people who look after us. We help people who help us. In short, we *care* about people who care about us."

There's that word again, Cameron thought. *Care.*

"The same is true in business," Gary went on. Cameron could hear the passion creeping into the young man's voice. "Our job here is to make sure everyone understands how very important they are to us, one customer at a time. We need to look for ways to make each of our customers' lives a little better—whatever that might look like. After all, if we can't find ways to be loyal to an individual customer, how can we expect an individual customer to be loyal to us?"

"I'm sure you have heard the term 'big data,' and how companies are using it to improve customer experiences?" Gary asked. Cameron nodded. They collected a lot of data at Household Solutions and were always looking for different ways to leverage it.

"Well," Gary said, "think of what we look after here as small data."

"Small data?" Cameron asked, raising an eyebrow.

"Yes," Gary replied. "You see, despite all the profiling and modelling one can do with big data, and the CRM tools that are available, they can never really create that visceral, emotional connection you get from a one-on-one interaction. That's why there is such a huge focus on customer service on the sales floor." Cameron nodded.

"So here, on this floor, we look for opportunities to work with customers on an even higher level. We try to really take ownership over their experience." He gestured for them to stand. "Here, let me show you what I mean."

Cameron and Madeleine stood and followed Gary to the far side of the expansive reception area. They stood discreetly beside a glass wall looking into a small boardroom. On one side of the boardroom table sat two women. One was younger, with short, streaked blonde hair. The other was somewhat older and, judging from her appearance, the younger woman's mother.

Standing at the other side of the table was a middle-age man with thinning brown hair, wearing a store name badge. In front of him were several large plastic shopping bags. One had a competitor's name emblazoned on it.

"That is Tanya," Gary whispered. "Her wedding is two weeks from now. It's quite big—somewhere around two hundred and fifty people. Her wedding theme is fruit. The bride and groom met when they were working together in a large orchard."

"The bride-to-be did all the planning and ordered a lot of the decorations and table settings from an online company. Unfortunately, she just found out last week the company will be unable to ship everything in time."

"Oh my goodness!" Madeleine exclaimed with her hand to her mouth. "That is so *horrible!*" Cameron nodded in agreement.

"It is," Gary agreed. "One of our employees down in the household decor department found out about it last week as Tanya and her mother were frantically looking for new table decorations. To their delight, they found some beautiful, elegant fruit baskets," Gary pointed to one on the boardroom table, "but we only had twenty-one of the thirty-three they were going to need.

"Our employee called up here and spoke to Tyler." Gary indicated the man in the boardroom. "Ty dug around, did some research, and called Tanya and her mother this morning to invite them in to see what he came up with."

Gary motioned them toward the boardroom door that was slightly ajar, and they all listened intently.

"Unfortunately," they heard Tyler say, "we found out that there was no way our supplier could get us more of these fabulous baskets in time for the wedding." The faces of the two women fell.

"But," he said with a smile, reaching for the plastic bag emblazoned with the competitor's logo, "I knew how much you liked them, so I tracked down the dozen more we needed at another retailer. Rather than just send you there—you already have enough on your minds—I took the liberty of purchasing them and bringing them in. They actually cost a little more at the other store, but we will sell them to you for the same price as the ones you bought from us. I hope this was okay."

Tyler reached into the bag and pulled out the baskets.

Tanya's eyes grew wide, and her mother put a hand to her mouth. "Really?" she asked. "You did that for us?"

"Of course!" Tyler said with a smile. "This *is* your wedding after all. I can't think of many things that are more important to get right!"

"But," Tanya's mother said, haltingly, "if you bought them from the other store for more than you're going to charge us, it means you're losing money. I don't understand."

"True," Tyler acknowledged with a big smile, "but your daughter is much more than just a transaction to us. She is a customer, a neighbor, a *person*—and one who is about to begin a whole new, exciting journey. That's more important than just a business transaction, don't you think?"

Both Tanya and her mother looked at each other, and then at Tyler in disbelief. Cameron was somewhat in disbelief as well.

He turned to Gary. "Wow. That's amazing. But at the risk of appearing a bit mercenary, I'm not sure I understand how this makes any business sense. If you did this with every customer, you would be out of business in no time."

Gary nodded in agreement. "Perhaps," he said, "but it actually does make business sense—on a couple of levels." He nodded toward the boardroom again.

"We also took the liberty of seeing if there was anything else we might be able to do to make your wedding special," Tyler said. "I know from our conversation that there were a lot of other things that also didn't arrive. If you are interested, I'd like to show you some of our ideas."

The two women nodded. Tyler reached into one of the other bags and pulled out a large, colorful, metal serving platter shaped like a giant strawberry, a package of flexible fridge-magnets, and a dozen permanent black markers. Each of the fridge magnets were shaped like a different fruit with a white space for writing a note.

"We thought that might be a really fun registration thing," Tyler said excitedly. "When people show up for the reception, they each get a fridge magnet. They use one of these permanent markers to write their well-wishes to you on the magnet, then stick it to the metal plate. Then, after the wedding, you have a great memento of the event!"

"That is such an awesome idea!" Tanya said with delight. Her mother agreed.

"Thank you!" they said in unison.

Tyler proceeded to present them with four more ideas, each received better than the last. When he was finished, Tanya's mother looked at him and said, "Wow! This is beyond anything we would ever expect. You people are truly amazing!" A beaming Tanya pulled her phone out of her purse and snapped a picture of all the fruit-themed ideas spread across the table. She tapped the keys for a few moments, then put the phone back in her purse.

"There," she said. "This *had* to go straight to Instagram!"

Cameron was nodding slowly as he watched the scene in the boardroom unfold. He turned to Gary. "Two women who will probably now shop in this store for life—plus a few of their friends; free advertising on social media; and an additional couple of hundred dollars in sales. Not a bad payoff for a few hours of someone's work and a small loss on a dozen baskets."

Gary nodded proudly. "*And*, we helped make someone's special day even more special," he said.

"Not bad at all," Cameron repeated softly, looking back through the glass into the boardroom. He lapsed into silence as he absorbed the lesson.

CHAPTER
THIRTY-SIX

THEY WALKED SLOWLY BACK to Gary's desk, and he told them about some of the other customers they had talked with that day. One was a man who had bought a reciprocating saw from their tools department and arranged for delivery. When it arrived, he noticed it wasn't the same saw he had picked out. He called to complain, and was told that they had actually given him a better brand that had even more features. A part-time employee in the shipping department learned they were going to be on sale in just a few days and had made the switch—so that the customer would get the better saw at an even better price. Needless to say, the customer was delighted.

Another was a long-time customer who was shopping for his wife's birthday, but his credit card was at its limit. The man had lost his job a few months back, Gary explained, and hadn't gotten back on his feet. When the cashier in the jewelry department couldn't complete the transaction, she notified one of Gary's colleagues. The customer was told there would be no charge for the two hundred dollar necklace. It was a gift from the store. The customer was also given an additional $100 gift card to help him through the tough times.

"He and his wife have been customers for over fifteen years," Gary explained before Cameron could ask. "They have spent a lot of money with us over that time. Given that they've always been there for us, it only seems right that we're there for them, doesn't it?"

Cameron wasn't convinced. "That's a pretty big precedent," he said doubtfully. "What if all of your customers suddenly started asking for the same treatment? Plus, there's no guarantees you'll ever see that money back."

Gary gave him an understanding look. "True. But that's the thing about loyalty, isn't it? It's given freely. You can't say 'I'll be loyal to you only if you are loyal to me.' That's not loyalty—that's a contract.

"Loyalty is about doing the right thing for the right reasons," he continued. "And we believe that if we are loyal to our customers, they will be loyal to us. We also believe that if a customer has been loyal to us, they deserve our loyalty. It's an integrity thing.

"I have also learned since working here," Gary said, "that people are not nearly as opportunistic as we fear. In fact, once you've created an emotional connection with customers, and they perceive you as an organization that genuinely cares about them, it's very rare that someone will take advantage of you."

Seeing no change in Cameron's skeptical expression, Gary continued. "Imagine, for example, that you see me give one stranger twenty dollars for parking because he didn't have his wallet with him. Would you turn around and ask me for twenty dollars, as well?"

"Probably not me," Cameron admitted. "But I'm sure there are some people who would."

"Sure, there are always a few," Gary conceded. "But very few. And we deal with those exceptions when they happen."

"I guess," Cameron said, "loyalty is like any other investment. There is a reward, but you have to be prepared to take the risk."

"Well said!" Gary said appreciatively. "For us, it's all about taking ownership and treating people like people. We try very hard not to think of customers as a group of people who buy things from us but instead as one individual at a time, and how we can make a difference in his or her life."

Cameron sat back to let this sink in. After a moment, he leaned forward and reached across the desk to shake Gary's hand. "Gary, I can't tell you how much your time has meant to me," he said sincerely. "One thing I know for sure is that you have definitely made a great difference in *my* life."

He rose, with Madeleine following suit. "I am so happy I could be of service," Gary responded, sounding very pleased indeed. He walked around the desk to shake Madeleine's hand, and watched with a smile as the two began walking back toward the elevators.

They had only gone a couple of steps when Cameron turned to his companion. "You have been uncharacteristically quiet," he said.

Madeleine looked up at him innocently. "Whatever do you mean?"

"No pointed questions?" Cameron asked, "No new instructions? No clever set-ups that make me look silly?"

Madeleine's eyes twinkled. "Oh, I *do* miss those!" she said with a laugh. "But truthfully, I'm not sure I have any left."

Cameron stopped and looked at her. "You mean we're done?" he asked in surprise. He suddenly realized that he was actually a little disappointed at the thought.

"Well," Madeleine said in response, "tell me what you've learned."

"All of it?" Cameron asked with a grin. "It might take a while."

Madeleine pushed the button on the elevator. The light above the door showed it was on the basement floor. "My guess is that you have a little over a minute," she said.

Cameron considered for a moment. "Well," he began, "it begins with understanding the customers' journeys—from the customers' points of view. Then we have to consider every customer touchpoint in the business to make sure that every policy, every process, and every practice is focused on creating the best possible experience.

"We have to be easy to do business with, and we have to genuinely care about the well-being and happiness of our customers. We have to set customer experience standards and constantly be assessing our performance against them—and at the same time looking for ways to continuously raise the standards.

"The most important element, though," Cameron said, absently looking at the ceiling as he drew on his memory, "is *people*. It is the people who directly and indirectly connect with our customers who really make the difference. We need Real People—not Gray People—and they need to be engaged, with the empowerment, tools, training, and direction to do what's right."

Cameron glanced at the elevator numbers. It was almost to their floor. He began to speak faster. "Which means none of it will happen without the right leadership in place. At every level we have to embrace the rules of Avi's garden. Customer experience has to course through the veins of the business. Everyone needs to understand that it's not just an add-on to what we do, it *is* what we do."

A bright chime sounded from the elevator, and the doors slid open. An elderly couple exited and walked toward the reception area. Cameron and Madeleine walked in. He was about to continue his review but stopped as he saw Madeleine push the button for the ground floor. He pointed to the button on the top labelled "MOM."

"Why on earth have they labelled this floor 'Mom'?" he asked, hoping to finally get an answer to his question. "That makes no sense to me at all."

Madeleine looked at it, as if noticing it for the first time. She laughed. "Oh, that's funny!" she said. "I guess the screw that's holding it must be loose." And with that, she reached up and spun the label right-side-up. It now read "WOW."

Cameron looked dumbly at the label, then back at Madeleine. "The WOW floor," he finally said. *Now* it made sense.

As the elevator started moving, Madeleine looked up at him expectantly. "You were saying?" she asked.

Cameron regrouped. "Right. So, wow customer experience is different than outstanding customer experience," he said. Madeleine smiled but said nothing. Cameron thought for a moment, then continued slowly as the concept began to crystalize in his head. "Outstanding customer experience is when everything is working together to create consistently positive experiences. It includes Processes, Policies, Practices, and People."

He thought for a second. "*Outstanding Customer Service* is the People part," he said finally.

He tapped the WOW plaque as he felt the elevator beginning to slow. "But *Wow Customer Experience* is different. Wow experiences are created when we take ownership. They happen when we focus on individuals, or on small data, as Gary referred to it. They are created when we recover from service failures, when we create unexpected positive outcomes, or when we turn negative situations into positive ones."

Cameron thought of Tanya and her mother, their disbelief in what the store had done for them, and Tanya's immediate response to post the experience on social media. Then his own observation that the experience had likely created customers for life resurfaced.

"Loyalty," Cameron said simply as the last piece of the puzzle fell into his brain. "The ownership, the personal connection, the sense customers have that we genuinely care about them—the wow things—these create loyalty." He recalled Gary's comments about real customer loyalty being created at an emotional and personal level.

A chime sounded, and the elevator doors opened. When Cameron looked over at Madeleine, he was surprised to see a brilliant beaming smile. She was proud of him, he thought. And that made him feel awesome.

"I think," she decreed, "this calls for a peppermint-frosted-choco-nana latte."

EPILOGUE

IT WAS A TUESDAY in mid-August, and at 8:30 in the morning the temperature in Los Angeles had already hit 85 degrees. Cameron sat under a multi-colored umbrella outside the Beverly Hills CappuGino's. *Deja-vu,* he thought, as he scanned the ever-present stream of people moving up and down the sidewalk.

He was feeling pretty good this morning. Not only were things going well at Household Solutions, but that morning he had discovered Chewbacca's invisible tormenter. It turned out that the sun coming in from the front window and the light from the lamps had been reflecting off his silver watch, creating an ever-moving, dancing image on the walls. Cameron had immediately taken the watch off, and although Chewbacca had eyed the walls suspiciously for a while, he was eventually satisfied that the threat was gone.

As he thought about this, he caught a glimpse of Madeleine walking airily down the street toward him. She was dressed in full Gypsy-garb. A gold-patterned, crimson scarf wrapped around her head was tied at the side and dangling loosely on her right shoulder. She'd paired a bright red, gold, and white bodice with a matching full-length, wrap-around, bohemian-style skirt and leather ankle boots. Swinging under her left arm was a large, soft, black leather purse.

Cameron stood as she approached. Madeleine opened her arms and gave him a long hug. "It has been FAR too long, young man!" she admonished with a big smile.

"Indeed it has," Cameron said in return. He stepped back to appraise her ensemble. "I would say I missed you, but I'm not sure anyone could ever miss you—no matter how big a crowd you are in!"

"Well, I do try to be outstanding whenever possible," she replied with an offhand flip of her wrist as she took Cameron's hand and sat down in the chair beside his. She looked at the two drinks already at the table, and her eyes grew wide. "What is THIS?" she asked excitedly.

"It is my newest creation!" came a voice from behind her. Madeleine looked around to see the wide smile of the restaurant owner. "Gino!" she said with delight.

"At your service, lovely lady," he said with a flourish. "And before you is a new frozen multi-swirl, blueberry-lemon-mint-chocolate-mocha with a maple-cinnamon straw." Madeleine let out a little squeak, grasped it with two hands, and brought the straw to her lips as though drinking out of a sacred chalice.

Her eyes grew wide. "Oh, *Gino*," she said breathlessly. "Oh, Gino—you have completely outdone yourself this time."

Gino bowed and raised his left arm toward Cameron. "In truth," he said modestly, "it was our friend's idea. He said that you deserved something very special. He was right, of course, so together we came up with this drink we have named the *Marvelous Maddy!*"

Cameron had never seen his eccentric friend fully blush before, but now her cheeks matched the crimson of her headdress. "I . . . I just don't know what to say!" Madeleine responded, still gazing at the drink clutched in her two hands.

"Now that, Gino, is truly a first!" Cameron said with a laugh, shaking the proprietor's hand. "We should relish this moment." Gino laughed with him, then turned back to Madeleine, who had begun delicately sipping her Marvelous Maddy.

"There is no one who has ever done more for me than you,"

Gino said sincerely. "From now on, this will be our signature drink—to honor the most beautiful lady in the world."

Madeleine looked up at Gino with a touched expression.

"And it doesn't hurt that it has also become Gino's best-selling drink by a country mile," Cameron chimed in, still smiling. "But I echo his thoughts. Maddy, you are amazing!"

A couple seated themselves at a nearby table, and Gino stood. "Ah, I am terribly sorry," he said to Cameron and Madeleine, "but I must excuse myself. I am on duty today, and I mustn't ignore my customers!" Without waiting for a reply, he spun and quickly made his way to the other table.

Madeleine looked at Cameron. The blush had disappeared, but there was dampness in the corners of her eyes. "The two of you give me far too much credit," she said to him. "You are both very bright young men." She took a breath, then locked his eyes with hers.

"But more importantly," she said to him, her voice rising a little, "tell me what is happening at Household Solutions! It's been almost five months, and I haven't heard a peep from you. What is going on? How is your progress? I am *totally* in the dark! *Which*, by the way, is devastating for a sensitive person like me."

Cameron grinned, and hung his head in mock-shame. He had, of course, kept her regularly updated via email, but this was the first opportunity he'd found to pry himself away from the office. It was also the first opportunity in a long time for Madeleine to scold him in person. "You're right, and I'm sorry," he said. "So much has happened in such a short time."

He took a sip of the Marvelous Maddy. "Where should I start?" he asked.

"Well, *not* from the beginning, that's for sure," Madeleine said with her eyes rolled up theatrically. "That would just be too painful to endure twice." Cameron had a brief flashback to her repeatedly banging her head against the table.

"Yes," he agreed. "For both of us."

"I'll start with my presentation to the leadership team," Cameron began, leaning forward in his chair. "As excited as I was with the plan I had created, I was still a little nervous about how they would respond."

"It turned out, however, that I had nothing to worry about. The activities I'd asked them to do at the beginning—assessing each department, embedding themselves with our customers, visiting stores—had already put them on a bit of a journey of their own. They were already starting to see glimpses of some of the things we experienced at the Saggezza Centre."

"Bottom line," he said with a satisfied smile, "they embraced the plan almost immediately. It was a bit rocky at first, but the leadership team was absolutely relentless—even Stan, who has turned out to be my biggest supporter."

"Rocky?" Madeleine asked, curiously.

"Yeah," Cameron said, leaning back in his chair. "The hardest part was cascading the message through the company, and I hadn't seen that coming. The managers and supervisors at the different levels had obviously not been part of the discussions at the beginning, so they didn't really embrace it at first. Most paid lip service to the idea of becoming more customer-centric, mind you, but they didn't really understand how much of a change it was going to be—and how much they would be expected to champion it. We really had to force the issue—almost to the point of micro-managing.

"It sounds horrible to say, but the turning point actually came a little over a month in, when we decided to weed the garden—and release four managers who had clearly decided not to get onboard. It eliminated some of the roadblocks, and it sent the message to everyone that we were serious about the new direction.

"Right after that happened," Cameron continued, "some of the people who had been sitting on the fence made serious commitments to change how they approached their roles. To our surprise, we actually had a couple of people—former direct-reports of the managers we let go—make a point to thank us for the decision. We even had over three dozen employees and managers email us to tell us how proud they were of the direction the company is headed.

"We decided to ramp up the messaging of our expectations throughout the company big-time," Cameron continued. Madeleine smiled at hearing the excitement in his voice. "We began a massive training initiative that both communicated the new direction and gave employees the skills to succeed.

"Susan, our VP of Human Resources, found a company that specializes in customer service training. They were amazing, and every single one of our employees has been through multiple workshops. Normally, we would have opted for something more like an e-learning approach—because of our size, and the significantly greater cost of external live training. But Susan convinced us having people together in an interactive setting provides far greater payoff when it involves people skills. She was absolutely right."

"Syd, our COO, had the most revolutionary idea," said Cameron. "I guess the experience he had while embedded with our customers really reinforced the idea of small data. He recommended that everyone in a management role at Household Solutions—from Gerard all the way to our managers-in-training—personally call at least three customers every day."

Madeleine lifted an eyebrow but said nothing.

"We get their names from our customer database," Cameron continued. "We call people up, introduce ourselves, tell them how much we appreciate them, and then just have a conversation. No questionnaires, no sales pitches—just conversations. We make notes of the details of the conversations and follow through on any action items that may come up. To date we have already made over twenty thousand calls!

"There was a lot of pushback at first, but the impact has been off the charts. Not only were we able to resolve over five hundred issues that customers hadn't bothered to report, but we estimate the calls have generated over a hundred thousand dollars in additional sales. It's just like what happened with Tanya's wedding!" he said enthusiastically.

Madeleine silently sat back in her chair with a wide smile.

"*And,*" Cameron went on, "much to our surprise, we got four viable new product ideas from our customers—things we had never thought of! They are in testing right now."

He leaned forward even more, looking straight at the smiling Gypsy in front of him. "Maddy, our sales have already started to go up, our pre-orders for Christmas have skyrocketed, our reviews on social media are changing for the better, and the employees throughout the company are happier than I have ever seen them.

"We haven't even started half of our initiatives," Cameron said. "I can't begin to imagine what will happen once the rest of them kick in."

He sat back suddenly in his seat, as though exhausted from his burst of adrenaline. "Maddy," he said, "I don't even know where to start thanking you."

"Oh, pish," Madeleine admonished, leaning forward with a dismissive hand-flip. "This was all *your* doing, young man. All I did was take you shopping."

Cameron grinned and rolled his eyes. "Yeah," he said. He knew better than to try and argue. "Shopping."

The two bantered back and forth for another half-hour until Madeleine looked at her watch and discovered she only had fifteen minutes to get to "an awesome, blockbuster sale at the Beverly Centre." As they rose to say their goodbyes, Cameron remembered something.

"Madeleine," he said, "I never did get a bill from you for everything you've done. Can you put one together for me?"

"I actually have it right here," Madeleine said as she fished through her huge purse. She pulled out a fuchsia-shaded envelope and handed it to Cameron. "It has, of course, already been paid," she said, "but here you go nonetheless!"

Already paid? Cameron wondered. He opened the envelope and looked at the single sheet of paper. There, handwritten, was an itemized list of all the shopping she had done courtesy of Cameron's credit card. At the bottom was a hand-drawn happy face, and a note that said, "Paid in Full." Cameron looked up at her.

"Fair enough," he said. "But from now on, you also get Household Solutions products free for life."

Madeleine's eyes grew wide. "Deal!" she said.

"Madeleine," Cameron said, turning serious for a moment, "any last words of advice?"

She thought for a moment and looked up at him with an equally serious expression. "Yes," she said. "There is one thing you must never forget." Cameron looked at her expectantly.

"Remember Avi's words," she said. "Complacency is the enemy. There is no end to this journey you have begun. The moment that you convince yourself you have arrived is the exact moment you begin the insidious descent to mediocrity. Be as vigilant with your customers as you would your dearest friend."

And with that, she leaned forward, pecked him on the cheek, and spun toward the Beverly Centre. The big purse was draped over her left shoulder, and her right arm was extended with forefinger thrust in the air making a circular motion. "When the going gets tough . . ." Cameron heard her say.

". . . the tough go shopping," he finished the thought quietly to himself.

ACKNOWLEDGMENTS

Wow. There are a lot of people to thank, and not nearly enough available pages. At a minimum, though, I need to acknowledge and thank:

- Jack David for setting me on the path of writing more than I ever intended; being an unwitting mentor; and for, in his own quiet way, smacking me upside the head when I need it the most.

- 18-year-old Jackie and Mary-Poppins-loving Margo for bringing Maddy to life.

- Yvette, for always supporting me on all of my journies

- Wade for the most awesome first proof a book ever had

- John, for instantly understanding what this book is to me.

- Everyone who has ever sat through one of my keynote presentations and workshops. Your insights and tough questions make me better. Your laughter and encouragement keep me alive.

Journey to WOW Resources for educators, trainers and coaches:

Additional insights and tools from The Journey to WOW are available, including exercises, discussion points, and strategies for embarking on your own journey.

To access these free resources, visit www.journeytowow.com

Shaun Belding speaking information

Shaun Belding is a popular keynote speaker on customer experience, customer service, leadership and creating an engaged workforce.

> To learn more, visit: www.shaunbelding.com
> To make an enquiry, contact: booking@shaunbelding.com

Outstanding Training Programs

Belding Training is the leading global provider of powerful, customized training on customer service, internal customer service, leadership and dealing with difficult situations.

> To learn more, visit: www.beldingtraining.com
> To make an enquiry, contact: info@beldingtraining.com

Customer Experience Consulting

The Belding Group can help you navigate your company's customer experience journey. Customer experience audits, In-depth strategic assessments and a results-focused plan.

> To learn more, visit: www.beldinggroup.com
> To make an enquiry, contact: info@beldinggroup.com

9 781633 936935